*To my precious gifts from God, Lucas, Jesse, and Devin; now that you are adults, is anyone paying you to fold your own socks?*

*To my lifelong partner in frugality, Randy; this is why we rolled pennies and hung our underwear to dry. I love you.*

# CONTENTS

# INTRODUCTION

I was disappointed to discover I couldn't fit everything I wanted to say into thirty chapters. Thirty looked like a good, solid number and sounded like perfect coverage for my topic; any more seemed long-winded and any less seemed unfinished. I tried to dismantle full chapters and hide bits of them throughout my content, cut yawn-stirring paragraphs (but couldn't find any), and delete anything that didn't add "oomph" to the book. After painstakingly searching and scrolling for days, my head pounded, the words jumbled before my eyes, and my brain felt like a radio between channels. My mind ached for clarity as I closed the laptop, shut my eyes, and hung my heavy head in my hands.

The silence was strange. The clickety-clack of the keyboard had become my music and its absence was deafening. My eyes flitted around the room, desperate to land on an object of inspiration. Time hung in the air like a bird hovering in a headwind and my discouragement was fierce.

And then I sensed it. Thirty-One. The ideal number. A wise number once given to a king from his mother; a priceless gift he then passed on to us. It's an influential number that speaks about marriage, finances, loving others, inner strength, and motherhood. *Everything* my story entails. Relief washed over me, my confidence soared, and I reopened my laptop to share this poetic piece with you.

### A Wife of Noble Character

*Who can find a virtuous and capable wife? She is more precious than rubies. Her husband can trust her, and she will greatly enrich his life. She brings him good, not harm, all the days of her life.*

*She finds wool and flax and busily spins it. She is like a merchant's ship, bringing her food from afar. She gets up before dawn to prepare breakfast for her household and plan the day's work for her servant girls.*

*She goes to inspect a field and buys it; with her earnings she plants a vineyard. She is energetic and strong, a hard worker. She makes sure her dealings are profitable; her lamp burns late into the night.*

*Her hands are busy spinning thread, her fingers twisting fiber. She extends a helping hand to the poor and opens her arms to the needy. She has no fear of winter for her household, for everyone has warm clothes.*

*She makes her own bedspreads. She dresses in fine linen and purple gowns. Her husband is well known at the city gates, where he sits with the other civic leaders. She makes belted linen garments and sashes to sell to the merchants.*

*She is clothed with strength and dignity, and she laughs without fear of the future. When she speaks, her words are wise, and she gives instructions with kindness. She carefully watches everything in her household and suffers nothing from laziness.*

*Her children stand and bless her. Her husband praises her: "There are many virtuous and capable women in the world, but you surpass them all!"*

*Charm is deceptive, and beauty does not last; but a woman who fears the Lord will be greatly praised.*

> *Reward her for all she has done. Let her deeds publicly declare her praise.*

—Proverbs 31:10-31

I don't have servant girls, spin flax, or dress in purple gowns, but I most definitely work hard, help the poor, and watch our finances. It took me forever to learn to laugh without fear of the future. The description of the woman found in Proverbs 31 is encouraging; it made me realize thirty-one wasn't such an inconvenient number after all and that I'd be honoured to have it in my book.

Thank you. Yes, you! Thanks for joining me on this roller coaster ride called "life." You will read about our family's ups, ups, ups of anticipation, the unexpected, head-banging turns appearing from virtually nowhere, and the downs that felt like the earth had dropped from beneath us. The pages are graced with everything from sassy, foot-stomping kids to finding unforeseen strength in the dark. You'll travel with us from childhood until today and hear my personal account of how I saved $100,000. There's more to life than bills, worrying about debt, and buying more *stuff*, and I can't wait to tell you all about it.

# IN THE BEGINNING

Chapter One

IF SOMEONE ASKED YOU IF YOU'D LIKE TO BE RICH, WHAT WOULD you say? Would your heart pound with excitement? Would you breathe a sigh of relief at the assurance of a better life? I'm sure we can all agree that given the chance, everyone questioned would have a different concept of what it means to be "rich." A destitute, single mother would jump for joy at the discovery of a forgotten ten-dollar bill in the pocket of her winter jacket whereas a powerful billionaire might crack a smile after his latest acquisition of a rare, classic car.

Although the criteria would differ from one person to the next, my own definition of being rich has graduated from the juvenile ideal of striving for popularity and driving a "look-at-me" car to a complete revelation that being a mother of three and having a devoted spouse to share my life with satisfies a desire in my heart that all the money in the world could never fill. So much so that four years ago my high school sweetheart and I celebrated our Silver Wedding Anniversary by renewing our vows and publicly thanking God for creating us for one another.

I squeezed into my original bedazzled wedding dress and as I started up the aisle of the church, the shocked smiles of our guests at its sky-high shoulder pads and eight-foot train created an instant cherished memory. Also surprised and sporting an ear-to-ear grin, my hubby Randy met me at the altar, tenderly kissed me on the cheek, and nodded for the pastor to begin.

Our ceremony included hand-written vows to "stop interrupting" (him), "tidy the bathroom counter" (me), and thankfulness for "doing laundry, killing spiders, and cleaning up dog poop" (both of us). We also acknowledged God provided us with similar views about money and appreciated we've always shared the same goals, even to this day, regarding our spending habits and financial values.

My honey and I were both raised in modest homes with sufficient worldly goods, primarily because our parents didn't blow their earnings on flashy cars and vacays to France. Our families didn't live to excess and their economic morals and standards were passed down to us. We both had part-time jobs as teens and like most adolescents, drained our bank accounts for high-top sneakers and neon mesh, boom boxes to record the now-forgotten mixed-tape, and all the yummy junk food we weren't permitted at home.

Growing up, I assumed our family was poor. I lived in a nice neighbourhood with a large yard and my own '70s velour-wallpapered bedroom, but because Mom and Dad weren't monetarily flamboyant or vain, I speculated, incorrectly, we were living paycheque to paycheque. We never owned a new car, routinely wore second-hand clothes, and couldn't possibly buy anything unless it was on sale. At the time, I had no idea my parents were introducing me to the well-grounded basis of my financial future, but little by little, I took it all in.

My mom and dad took us on a few fun-filled vacations to Florida when I was a teen. The flashbacks of driving three never-ending days, from sunup to sundown, playing hour after agonizing hour of the license plate game, is forever burned into my brain. But so are the incredible memories of being in a different country for the first time, experiencing the gradual warmth on the highway due south, and getting to shake hands with Mickey Mouse!

For our first trip, my parents made a deal with my baby brother, younger sister, and I; in order to go on our Floridian Family Adventure of a Lifetime, we kids had to contribute to the cost of the trip. This only added another reason as to why I believed we were a dollar or two less than well-off. I wasn't old enough to comprehend our help wasn't exactly needed to pay for the road trip and they were teaching their beloved offspring that if we wanted *things* we had to work hard and save, save, save.

In attempts to earn a bit extra, one day my mom loaded us three kids and a stack of stinky burlap bags into our old station wagon and transported us to the untamed wilds of the deep, dark forest (truthfully, only twenty minutes from our home). She then proceeded to instruct her young brood how to harvest lycopodium. Huh? That's what I thought too. Lycopodium is a short, evergreen plant that was often used to make Christmas wreaths and is now a common homeopathic remedy. It only took a nanosecond before I decided I positively loathed picking lyco! It was tedious, backbreaking work and there were millions of terrifying bugs and spiders hiding in the undergrowth, just waiting for the opportunity to frighten my pre-teen body into an adrenaline-inspired freak-out.

I was beyond perturbed that my own mother, the one person in the universe who was supposed to protect me from life-threatening danger, would subject me to such torturous child labour. Furthermore, I was incensed that because I was the oldest, I was expected to work at an efficiently rapid rate while my four-year-old brother got to frolic around the thicket looking like an adorable, blonde cherub. I caught on very quickly that the faster I filled my bag, the sooner I got to get the heck out of those petrifying, insect-infested woods!

The Lyco truck came through town every Saturday and our output got weighed and tagged. We only received a painfully small amount of compensation per bag—which hardly seemed worth it to a 12-year-old me—but gradually, week after week, we saw our savings grow. My mom constructed a large chart where we kept close track of our earnings, and our slow, yet steady monetary accomplishment fueled my motivation to keep on picking. Visibly seeing our progress in thick, dark ink only elevated the enthusiasm of our first big trip and I had no clue, and was very annoyed by it in the moment, that my parents were implanting my core concepts about budgeting and wealth.

*Things* aren't free. You must work hard. Don't take your earnings for granted. Save your money. Watch your expenditures and teach your children to do the same. Take serious measures to avoid debt and be thankful for what you have rather than always wishing for something better. I'm not too proud to eat a slice of sour humble pie and admit that even though I thought I did at the time, my inexperienced self didn't quite know everything.

I'm eternally grateful for having been educated in the art of wise money management at such an early, impressionable age and the remembrance of my first real vacation is still fondly etched in my mind.

All told, I've saved the Leighton family more than $100,000 in the past three decades by being a savvy saver and careful spender. We've made many mistakes along the way, and I presume God probably smiled and shook His head in disbelief a few times, but we've learned from them and continued to move forward.

Please don't be disappointed to discover this book isn't a financial bible that will give specific instructions on how to get rich quick! Instead, you'll join me on a deeply emotional and physical account of the miserable misfortunes and conservation concepts that shaped our family. Today we can profess fearlessness but our spiritual and financial growth process certainly wasn't pretty and it surely wasn't quick.

# GETTING STARTED

Chapter Two

Right after we married, Randy and I picked up a dog-eared book at a garage sale about becoming economically independent. It was a common sense guide with detailed suggestions about budgeting, wise spending, and saving for retirement. As newlyweds, our incomes were practically nonexistent and we did anything we could to stretch our dollar, so this book was a welcome addition to our minimalist mindset.

Randy and I poured over the book like it was the Bible while our actual Holy Bible collected dust on the shelf. Ouch. We acquired the necessary knowledge to allot for bills, plan our purchases, avoid debt, and invest for retirement. We outlined our checklist and implemented everything we read. That well-loved book was the first step on our married journey that brought us to the relaxed economic life we have today, and I can't fathom how we would have financially succeeded without it.

As the babies came and the bills got bigger, I worried about money. Excessively fretful would have better described my attitude of unwillingness to trust God and rely on Him to meet all our needs. Early in our marriage, we thought we were the masters of our own destiny, we could take care of ourselves, and we only needed God for the most disastrous of times. My goodness, we couldn't have been more mistaken and rue the day we ever felt we didn't need God as the source of our wisdom, our provision, our foundation, and our strength.

Thankfully, our Heavenly Father is merciful and patient and forgave us our naiveté and faults. As all loving parents do when children are stubborn, He gently let us make the mistakes we were so insistent upon making and allowed us to face the consequences of our actions. We eventually learned to ask God to guide us through our tough choices and He filled our lives with more goodness than we could ever possibly have attained ourselves.

It would be many years and challenging life lessons before I truly understood and accepted the concept of God's blessings. Randy and I discovered His favour has been monumental in both our marriage and the raising of our children. While we are thrilled by the gifts and benefits we've physically seen over the years, we are blown away by our belief He has also cared for us in ways we know nothing about.

Like the old country song "Unanswered Prayers," God has a very special way of loving us. When we're running late and have to run back into the house three times, that's God protecting us from a fender bender. When we're turned down for a job we begged for, that's God shielding us from a toxic work environment. When we're fired up but hold our tongue from giving a heated reply, that's God stopping us from becoming a person we don't want to be. Unanswered prayers can be a blessing in disguise and can also save our lives!

When we finally realized what it meant to be #blessed, and shifted from a perspective of mild appreciation to a deep, unwavering thankfulness, our whole viewpoint changed, not only with regard to our bank account, but spiritually as well.

Our circumstances and marriage haven't always been easy; there were numerous times over the years when my husband and I nearly lost all hope. But a gradual transformation of our mindset introduced us to a profound gratitude we hadn't known before. We began expressing to others all God had done for us, using Psalm 9:1 as our guide, *"I will praise you, Lord, with all my heart; I will tell of all the marvelous things you have done."*

My soulmate and I faithfully tithed (donated to our church) for many years before one day developing a powerful desire to increase the amount we were giving. God wants us to share all we have with others and depend on Him to supply what we need, and even though we always tithed a little something, we didn't always do so cheerfully. We gave because we felt obligated to, not because we really felt called to. We selfishly held on to what little we had in case we ever met with an unforeseen shortage, with no inkling that when we take care of God's people, He takes care of us.

While no one was actually telling us we weren't tithing and giving enough to charity, I sensed it in the depth of my soul and knew serious changes were immediately required. The Apostle Paul tells us,

> *Remember this—a farmer who plants only a few seeds will get a small crop. But the one who plants generously*

*will get a generous crop. You must each decide in your heart how much to give. And don't give reluctantly or in response to pressure. "For God loves a person who gives cheerfully." And God will generously provide all you need. Then you will always have everything you need and plenty left over to share with others.*

—2 Corinthians 9:6-8

Our family's attitude was in need of a major adjustment. Over time, we started not only feeling, but seeing as well, a difference in our blessings, both financially and spiritually. It was quite a while, and many wake-up calls later, before we grasped and fully understood we were to put *all* our faith in God. For everything. Paul, in his letter to the church in Philippi said, *"And this same God who takes care of me will supply all your needs from his glorious riches, which have been given to us in Christ Jesus"* (Philippians 4:19).

Randy and I have encountered true fiscal losses over the past 29 years, but it's only within the past few years we've had the ability to comprehend that our future always has been, and always will be, in God's hands. We are sorry it took us so long to catch on to that and we really do appreciate God's patience with us. We trust Him to provide for us and finally see what we've lost monetarily has been made up in spiritual blessings—three of which are our kids; Lucas, Jesse, and Devin, who we initially thought we'd never get the chance to meet.

# BABY BLISS

Chapter Three

PREPARE YOURSELF FOR NEVER-BEFORE-HEARD WISDOM, revelation, and insight on how to raise babies and be filthy rich at the same time! I apologize for being the bearer of bad news, but that concept is an absolute fairy tale.

After enduring the prolonged anguish of infertility, God graciously granted us a viable pregnancy and we were overcome with joy. Randy and I were the same as any expectant young parents, blindly trudging through all the unicorns and rainbows, ecstatically preparing for baby Leighton's arrival. We drafted our must-have list and thanked our mothers and fathers for helping us check off the stroller and crib. Practical gifts are always well-received and those large additions allowed us to save for the lesser things.

A newspaper flyer stated Sears was having a "Baby Sale" and we gleefully forked over $200 we had diligently saved on miniature undershirts, crisp yellow crib sheets, furry warm sleepers, and a frilly bassinet. Friends and relatives joined in the excitement of our impending parenthood and hosted a small baby shower for us, adding welcome essentials to our mini-collection of whatever a newborn might use. We didn't have much in the way of an expendable income back then so rather than spend more money, I lovingly hand-sewed bumper-pad covers and quilted balloon decorations for the nursery walls.

Because of our low income and the ridiculous price of disposable diapers, my mother suggested I give cloth diapers a try and bought me my first pack of brilliantly coloured, soft-as-a-baby's-bottom, Velcro-fitted diapers. I wasn't sure I was prepared for the tiresome commitment of cloth diapers—the more frequent changing and excessive washing and folding—but it wasn't long before I got the hang of it and my heart sang cheerfully every time I saw the lengthy expanse of darling diapers on the rickety old clothesline out back.

What started as an idea to save a buck or two, turned out to be huge savings over the years and covered the three tiny bums belonging to our handsome sons Luc and Jes, and our beautiful daughter Devin. While we still used throwaway diapers for outings and faraway car trips, the cloth diapers—which didn't end up so troublesome after all—proved to be an effective method of preserving our money, or lack thereof, for more pressing and imperative needs like food, our car, and rent!

I also saved a whopping amount over the years by breastfeeding our beloved blonde angels. Although bottle-feeding seemed preferential to me at first, the only reason I gave nursing a shot was because it was free. Neither Randy nor I had been breastfed as a baby, I didn't have any close girlfriends that had nursed their children, and I wasn't in close contact with even one woman that was in the process of breastfeeding.

Breastfeeding wasn't nearly as popular in 1994 as it is today, so I felt desperately alone on my quest to conserve our cash. After a bit of a rocky start, with absolutely no hands-on support, my precious infant son and I got into the swing of things and it wasn't any time at all before I fell deeply and passionately in love with breastfeeding. Not only was I saving our wee clan thousands of dollars in formula costs, but it was also incredibly convenient and exceptionally simple. Luc, Jesse, and Devin were all blissfully breastfed and I was happy I could nurse anywhere, any hour of the day as a stay-at-home mommy, without the fuss of powders, bottles, and refrigerators.

I'm pretty sure I was considered an old-fashioned pioneer by my friends and family (or possibly even weird) due to the occasional raised eyebrow or quizzical glance. Not only did I not know of any families who utilized cloth diapers and opted to breastfeed, I certainly wasn't personally aware of any mama who made her own baby food. After buying our first grocery basket of astronomically-priced commercial baby food, I was sure I could somehow, in some way, make the exact same meal for a fraction of the cost.

I didn't have access to the Internet back then, I couldn't find a book at the library on do-it-yourself baby food, and Baby Bullet hadn't been invented yet, so I blended a variety of grown-up food and prayed for the best. I froze delectable pureed portions of beef stew and turkey rice casserole in ice cube trays for convenience and easy preparation, and my tots showed their appreciation by kicking their little feet and clapping their chubby hands every time they saw the spoon coming. Our children were fed regular food from very early on in their babyhood and one of my life's biggest regrets is that I didn't introduce them to broccoli and asparagus sooner!

As my hubby and I became more conscious of the content of processed and factory-prepared food over the years, I'm so relieved I breastfed and offered my children whole, preservative-free, made-with-love, real food. Homemade baby food was far more economical than commercial baby food; it saved our one-income entourage plenty, and was a much healthier option for them too.

As we were still a fairly young couple with three gorgeous babies born in less than three years, we didn't really have a huge stash of savings or investments. Randy had been having a small pre-authorized withdrawal taken from his payroll for a few years and we had a very meager nest-egg of a registered retirement savings plan (RRSP). Shortly after Devin was born, we started having an additional $25 taken off each bi-weekly paycheque and placed into a savings bond. While a separate bank account would have been another feasible option, our money was safer in the bond as we didn't have everyday access to it and couldn't dip into it for unnecessary things.

We knew that the ideal function of the bond was to leave it in its specified location until it reached maturity but we opted to use it for a different and remarkably effective purpose. Every December, we'd redeem the accrued $600 and use it for our anniversary and Christmas spending. It seemed like a free reward to us and protected us from having a large unexpected credit card bill at the beginning of January. This strategy worked for us for a long time and it was miniature practices like this that led us directly onto the path of our first big purchase.

# MOVIN' ON UP

Chapter Four

FOR THE FIRST SEVEN YEARS OF OUR MARRIAGE, WE RENTED ONE of the Permanent Married Quarters (PMQs) available to Randy as a member of the Canadian Armed Forces. While we loved the camaraderie and closeness of our military community, we were truly eager for a little home of our own.

After serving his first nine years as a soldier in the same location, my groom was posted to a new military base four months after Devin's birth. Unfortunately for us, the federal government was in the process of selling the PMQs to a private corporation and we were forewarned the rental fees would be increasing. After a bit of research, we saw that housing market prices were fairly low and they gave us the push we needed to purchase our first home.

Randy received a well-deserved promotion with his posting and we combined his salary increase with our cashed-out RRSPs under the Home Buyer's Plan and bought our first house in July 1997. It was a small duplex on a beautifully-treed lot and was a practical and picturesque area in which to raise our three young children. We were thrilled our sacrifices paid off and were ecstatic to finally have a place to call our own.

My honey and I reminisce on that time and know God was walking beside us, quietly watching and waiting for us to turn to Him. My Gramma started taking me to church when I was eight years old and I went every Sunday until I got married. Sadly, in the first few years of our marriage, I became a holiday Christian and only participated in church services when we travelled to visit relatives. We did not regularly attend any church and we didn't take our children either. We only tithed when necessary and usually only an amount we deemed would appease God, not please Him.

We occasionally lost sleep about money—well mostly me, my husband, not so much—and were very conscientious of our saving and spending. We viewed ourselves in complete control of our financial future and were cruising along nicely, albeit minimally, in our economic objective. We paid our bills, didn't amass debt, and made an effort to save where we could. While we weren't selfish in any way and were generous with others, we had absolutely no idea God governed every aspect our lives, including our marriage and our bank account.

While I still prayed and loved God, I definitely wasn't anywhere close to the woman I aspired to be. I wanted my actions to be the proof that God exists, He is good, and with Him it's possible to have a peaceful life free from fear of the unknown. I've come so spiritually far since the early days of our marriage and I can't believe I allowed such a lengthy period of time to pass before making God my primary focus and putting Him in His rightful place of honour. It's not like I turned into a bad person or strayed too far away from what I learned in Sunday School, I just didn't know how to place my assurance in His wisdom and love, and my fears and lack of faith proved it.

After purchasing our home and suffering a severe bout of postpartum depression, I started to stumble my way back toward God. I had tried to do everything on my own for so long that I felt like I was on a never-ending road with no map, no compass, and no destination in sight. My heart contained a fierce longing like I'd never known before, with an empty loneliness impressing upon me that I couldn't do life by myself. I was in desperate need of God's guidance and quickly came to accept that He had been walking beside me all along; He'd always had His hand out and was just patiently waiting for me to take it.

One of my Gramma's favourite hymns was written by C. Austin Miles in 1912 and is titled "In The Garden."

*And He walks with me and He talks with me,*
*And He tells me I am His own.*
*And the joy we share as we tarry there,*
*None other has ever known...*

I took His hand and started taking our crew to church. We increased our giving a touch and warmed a pew on Sundays for appearance's sake but regrettably weren't dedicated to developing a full-on relationship with God and figuring out what His good plan was for us for many years to come.

He wants to be first in our thoughts because when He is, we think less of ourselves and more about those that hunger to see and be impacted by God's love. When we take our minds off our wants for a few minutes, we see the lost, the broken, and the countless desolate people all around us, hopelessly aching for an encouraging word and a fresh start. That's our purpose. And even though the postpartum depression really took its toll, I discovered my other calling, the most gratifying one of my life.

# THE EARLY YEARS

Chapter Five

"MOMMY," THE SWEETEST WORD I'VE EVER HEARD. WHILE MY high school friends were completing university applications and planning prestigious careers, I daydreamed about marrying my cute boyfriend and having a nursery full of toddlers. After only one year of university, I decided it wasn't for me, Randy proposed, and we were married six months later.

We slipped into our new roles as Mr. & Mrs. without a hitch and started trying for a little one to share our love with right away. Although conceiving took a number of seemingly endless and frustrating years, God graciously blessed us with three energetic and miracle babies.

We never had to foot the bill for daycare over the years as my better half and I never questioned I would be a stay-at-home mommy. My soldier's profession often took him out on maneuvers for weeks, even months on end, and it was important to us that one of us always be home with the children.

But caring for a one-, two-, and three-year-old, day in and day out, is flat-out exhausting, so to give myself a brief respite from always having to pee with the bathroom door open, I picked up a part-time, evening job at a nearby restaurant. But after paying a babysitter (who struggled under such a heavy workload anyway), my measly paycheque hardly seemed profitable. And on top of that, I usually spent my whole shift worrying about my kids and missing them terribly, so I weighed the pros and cons and happily left the job.

It became my mission to see how many things I could do in our town that didn't cost a cent. I took my munchkins to the beach, had yummy picnics in the park, went to the library, and visited the playground almost daily. The kids were having a blast but I was agonizingly lonely. I was still suffering some of the lingering ramifications of depression and was dying for a friend.

I was overjoyed to see a flyer at the library for a Moms and Tots group I thought would be perfect for us. I assumed my children would have other kids to play with and

I would get the much-needed adult connection I'd been profoundly craving. It turned out to be one of the most painful experiences of my life and it, without question, shaped and remoulded me into the person I am today.

The first time I took the children to Moms and Tots was alright, I guess. The facilitator introduced herself as the kids took off to play with the toys. She quickly showed me around the room and then headed to her desk to do paperwork. There were a few mamas huddled in the kitchen area, deep in conversation, and after checking on my children, I gathered up the courage to introduce myself and made my way over for a coffee. As I politely said "excuse me" to reach the paper cups, one of the women glanced my way and gave me a thoroughly disdainful once-over.

The sick sensation in my stomach was instantaneous as the mood in the room shifted from what I'd perceived as welcomingly pleasant to cold and uninviting. Disheartened, I timidly introduced myself anyway, hoping I was only imagining the woman's immediate distaste for me. She gave a curt "hi," without reciprocating her name, and promptly turned her back to me, resealing the tight circle I'd interrupted. Her newly hushed tone was evidence of my rejection, as was the fact the other two women didn't even acknowledge me at all. I was devastated.

All my hopes and dreams of making a new friend were shattered in a split second. I tried to tell myself maybe they were having an imperative, life-or-death discussion but as more moms entered the room, they all flocked eagerly into their private club and I was left to play with the children.

My kids were in their glory with all the new, exciting toys but as I begrudgingly sat with them on the geometric shape carpet, tears filling my eyes, all I could think was that I didn't *want* to play with my kids. We came to the play-group so I could get a break from them and my only wish in the entire world, at that precise moment, was to be a welcomed part of that horrible clique.

As I silently cried in the car all the way home, I realized all wasn't lost. The rear view mirror reflected the three beaming faces of my angels who were enthusiastically asking when we could go back. And although I would have preferred to never set foot in that awful place again, I always did everything I could to enhance the well-being of my children and ensure they had every opportunity for happiness, even if it meant sacrificing my own.

I swallowed my insecurities and pasted on a fragile smile when we returned the following Tuesday. Continuing my friend quest, I tried to engage a few women in conversation but no matter how hard I tried, week after week, I just couldn't fit in. I'd always had good friends in high school and Randy and I were part of a large circle of army buddies at our former posting, and frankly, I just couldn't comprehend why this elite cluster of moms didn't want me in their circle.

Then, at the end of our first month, I became acutely aware that all their husbands worked in prestigious, high-paying, white-collar careers at a nearby laboratory and blue-collar families—apparently that was us—didn't really meet the prerequisite qualifications to be a part of their royal set.

I could plainly see all the ladies were dressed in Ralph Lauren and carrying ridiculously expensive diaper bags; their offspring were dressed in button-downs, church dresses, and leather oxfords (to a play group, seriously?), and my kids were just in their Pooh Bear track suits and hand-me-down sneakers. The room looked like a photo shoot for a GapKids commercial and my children, while positively precious, looked embarrassingly out of place.

Evidently it mattered, but why? My kids shared the toys and used their manners at the snack table. A stranger's net worth didn't matter to me so why did it matter to these girls? I've never forgotten that Moms and Tots group and the damage it did to my sense-of-self. I couldn't see it then, but, *"And we know that God causes everything to work together for the good of those who love God and are called according to his purpose for them"* (Romans 8:28).

It all came full circle many years later when I ended up working for a Moms and Tots centre myself. Over time, my life's mission statement had become "Let my actions improve the day of every person I meet." I treated every woman that came through the door of the playgroup with respect and as an equal. It didn't matter to me if they had a low income, an impressive occupation, a run-down Toyota, or a deluxe SUV, they were all there for the same reason and I made absolutely sure everyone felt welcome.

As sad as it was, that crippling incident as a desperate young mother turned out to be an advantage for me. God took an ugly situation and transformed it into something beautiful. I owe Him so much gratitude for walking beside me during those isolated and lonely years and I know I benefitted from my experience as it propelled me into the passionately intuitive and sympathetic person I am today; a light of hope shining like a beacon into the lives of others.

# SAVVY SAVING

Chapter Six

THE CUTE POOH BEAR TRACKSUITS MY BABIES WORE AT MOMS and Tots were a gift from their aunt. My honey and I relied on birthdays and Christmas for new clothes for the kids, but for ourselves, we shopped at thrift stores. Back then, vintage and previously-loved was starting to become more popular but wasn't nearly as trendy as it is today. Luc, Jes, and Dev always looked presentable when we went out, but at home we always just wore our threadbare play clothes, including me.

Like many parents, Randy and I rarely bought anything for ourselves and just didn't see the point in living to excess. Restaurants were saved for special occasions like birthdays and anniversaries and we never ordered takeout. We bought all groceries on sale, I almost always used coupons and cooked from scratch and I continually looked for ways to stretch our buck as far as it would go. We'd buy a bushel of apples every fall and the kids and I would make enough cinnamon applesauce to freeze for the entire winter. We had the smallest cable television package available, never bought lottery tickets, utilized the library for magazines instead of subscribing, bought a tub of ice cream for an indulgence rather than visiting the ice cream parlour, and went camping for summer vacations as opposed to paying for flights and hotels.

Don't get me wrong. We did spend money. I'd sporadically let the children pick out a new book or puzzle at the discount store and Randy and I would occasionally rent a movie on a Saturday night. We'd sometimes share a large fry from the chip truck and once a year bought a round of mini-golf during summer break. We were always grateful for our spare change jar that afforded us a few small luxuries but never forgot to consider them treats, and that's what made us savour them so much more.

By our tenth wedding anniversary, we were paying down our mortgage as rapidly as we could and still contributing to both the RRSPs and the yearly savings bond. With another increase in Randy's salary, we were able to start an education fund for our children. In hindsight, we may have been investing a tad more than we ought to have been as things were pretty tight more often than not. Like many families, we had to wait until payday to get groceries, but on more than one occasion, I had to take change out of the kids' piggy banks just to buy them some milk!

We were just about to lower the amount of our RRSP deposits when God—who is *always* on time and in control—brought a part-time, unexpected babysitting job my way. I love that He knows what we need, exactly when we need it. To this day, I never cease to be impressed by God's power and His indescribable love for His children. God is so awesome! Caring for another wee guy the same age as my son enabled us to keep up with our financial obligations and still have a teeny bit extra to spare.

While our dedication to our budget never allowed us to grab takeout coffee, buy a new shirt on a whim, or get away for a night "just because," it did allow Luc, Jesse, and Devin to be involved in a number of activities. It was essential to us to keep them both physically and socially active and we strived to always set enough aside to shower them with fun and rewarding opportunities.

Swimming lessons were a no-brainer as our warmer months were traditionally spent at the lake and summer day camp was always a hit as the kids took great pleasure in bellowing their slapstick camp songs at the end of the one week we could afford every year. Randy and I were the leaders of our church youth group and although it was free for kids to attend, we looked after most of the resources necessary to feed them yummy suppers, play rowdy games, and go ice skating. Our children loved the recreational aspect of the group and we're glad we instilled the Christian values in them they still hold today.

And then there was hockey. My hubby was constantly on the hunt for second-hand gear and I always made sure to have lots of snacks on hand so we wouldn't have to eat out. The kids got their physical activity, learned to work as a team toward a common goal, and we were always together as a family. It was a win-win situation and even though we were utterly exhausted for so many years, we have absolutely no regrets.

# WHAT'S OUR WORTH?

Chapter Seven

WHEN WE FIRST START OUR COMMITMENT TO THE BEAUTIFUL life God has to offer, we are as rough and raw as freshly mined gemstones; our harsh outer layer concealing the priceless jewel of our soul. After we express our devotion to God and His truth, Jesus helps us become a new creation and the Holy Spirit takes up permanent residence in our lives and teaches us the way. The Trinity holds us as coarse and uncultured rocks and lovingly sets to work. They begin by chipping away our sharp and unsuitable edges.

Pride, gossip, selfishness, negativity, envy, and unforgiveness are just some of the traits that have no business in a Christian's life. As time passes, our jagged edges are polished away and a radiant gleam begins to rise to the surface. God, Jesus, and the Spirit work in harmonious unison with each one, tenderly loving it—with more grace than any human can comprehend—into a glorious work of the utmost brilliance.

Occasionally it only takes a few months, but more often than not, the chiseling process takes years of precise and diligent handiwork. Much of our reshaping happens when we find ourselves in circumstances that range from mildly annoying to downright dreadful. And even though it feels unbearable to us, God produces His best results when we're in a brutally tough crisis; the occurrences that feel like our head is about to explode in shocking devastation and we can't possibly take one more step forward. We have no choice but to cry out to Him and He warmly responds with merciful compassion.

Because we live in a sin-filled world, Christians still undergo the same catastrophic earthly events as others, but we gradually learn to adapt to them in different ways. We become more accepting of God's plan, more faithful in His pure love for us, more tolerant of the fluctuations between life's natural highs and lows, and more adept at finding light in the murky shadows of our surroundings.

In God's affection for His treasures, more and more magnificent light shines through and He begins to use it as an example to others who remain in their untouched state.

Each are exceptional in their own way, there are no two alike, and with practice they exhibit the divine fruits given to them by the Holy Spirit: love, joy, peace, patience, kindness, goodness, faithfulness, gentleness, and self-control. God also supplies them with special and unique gifts to show all those around them that honour and decency really do exist within this grim and aching mankind.

God's family is overflowing with exquisite masterpieces and yet miraculously, always has room for more. He uses His cultivated gems as models of His outstanding workmanship and lines up opportunities for them to share their testimony and personal account of their transformation. Amid life's ordeals, adversities, and teachings, God continues to shine and bring luster to each one until it is as pure as possible here on earth.

During our refinement process, the Holy Spirit is ever-present, gently blowing away our impurities, softly guiding and counseling us toward the truth. Jesus is always available for us to talk to; He hears our sorrow and desires, and lovingly goes to the Father on our behalf.

My walk with God has been an extended journey with many ebbs and flows. He was right beside me in my loneliest valleys and cheered me on when I scaled my mountains.

I started out as a very damaged and flawed stone that God never gave up on. I was adamant I could do everything on my own and because of my pride, my progression took years longer than necessary.

With each painful cut of every ragged edge, God held me tightly in His hand and brought me into a deeper relationship with Him. While I couldn't understand God's methods during my times of sanctification, much of His expertise is falling into place in my mature years, and I can see, with complete clarity, how many of my wearisome issues led me to the unparalleled contentment I possess today.

I'm honoured to say I now put God first in every aspect of my life. Although bookstores are teeming with self-help guides, His Word (the Bible) is the only book on the planet that offers me the best possible outcome for my life and I aspire to live by its truth every day. God has a good plan for me; not a plan of disaster, but one of hope.

I'll continue to run the race He's prepared for me and one day I'll triumphantly cross the finish line, arms raised and face beaming, knowing I've conquered it all. We don't possess the skill or superhuman powers required to master our existence alone, but with God all things are possible. It may sound odd but I now respect having had my abrasive and sinful edges chipped away which more often than not, occurred while I was learning from my mistakes.

# MESSY MISTAKES

Chapter Eight

We all make mistakes and then endure their consequence while hopefully not making the same poor choice again. Mistakes are an invaluable method of determining the difference between a choice that didn't work out the way we had intended and an option that would have had a much healthier outcome. From the very start of our marriage my groom and I conserved our money, a practice that's proved to never be a mistake.

Randy and I both believe, with our whole hearts, that God created us for one another. As a young girl, I prayed for a boyfriend that would eternally love me as much as I loved him and gratefully, Randy vows that he loved me before we even had our first date—thank you, Jesus! We cherish our compatibility regarding our shared passion for travel, the ability to enhance one another's strengths and be supportive of each other's weaknesses, our fierce commitment to fidelity, dedication to our children, and a mutual pursuit to be practical with our incomes. God brought us together knowing life wouldn't be easy, but that together we'd make it work.

I wouldn't say Randy and I were ever "cheap" because that just concocts a vision of oddballs who ration toilet paper. But in order not to misuse our hard-earned wages, we used to buy the cheapest products we could find: the lowest quality dish soap, towels, and batteries, and the least expensive toys, vacuum bags, and windshield washer fluid. And we found out—the hard way—that budget merchandise doesn't always offer the best value.

In order to preserve what we had by purchasing the most inexpensive household goods we could find, we slowly caught on to the reality we were actually wasting our precious cash in doing so. We learned research is a very effective method of ensuring things will last long-term, especially when making large purchases like washing machines and used cars. Even if we're paying somewhat more at the outset, better quality products tend to last above and beyond their poorly-made counterparts.

Ironically, some higher-priced items aren't better than middle-of-the-road ones; you just pay for the brand name and the pride of being enslaved to the latest craze. Today, we have the ability to Google any item on the planet and instantly read its reviews; it pains my spouse and I to say we wasted money over the years by trying to save it, but we're appreciative to have gained the wisdom.

We've owned many used cars over the years and have prayed, repeatedly, that God would bless us with the perfect car, at the right time, with a great price that would suit our specifications. By committing that specific request to God, we've experienced sensational success with used vehicles throughout our marriage and I pray we'll continue to do so for many years to come.

I'm pretty sure our children had the same misguided impression of our financial state as I did about my parents when I was a kid. Growing up, I was under the assumption I was poor because of my mom and dad's savvy and frugal spending habits and one time, when our daughter was about nine years-old, it became evident to Randy and I that our kids thought we were one step away from living in destitution.

We'd come out of the arena after hockey practice and Devin saw her teammate getting into his dad's flashy new truck—a massive truck; a shiny, redder-than-a-fireball, larger-than-life, monster of a truck. As we were climbing into our previously-owned, little-bit-rusty, well-loved, and well-used family van, Devin said, "I wish you and Daddy could afford a cool truck like that."

Jesse laughed and Luc rolled his eyes and said, "As if."

I looked at her, square in the face and replied, "We *can* afford a truck like that."

My sons' smirks quickly vanished and they all looked at me, dumbfounded and speechless.

I informed my children we could afford a truck like that if we wanted to. We could afford a vehicle payment of more than $600 each month if we wanted to, but we didn't want to! Then I taught them about debt. I defined investing, explained about savings and pointed out instead of us owning a glitzy red truck, we'd been to Walt Disney World, twice. It was an opportunity to teach my children a pivotal truth that day. Although our wealth appeared to be invisible, we definitely weren't poor.

Because of our cautious habits we had just opened our first tax-free savings account, had reserves for unexpected emergencies, held an education fund for our kids, and had amassed a flourishing investment portfolio. I'd been back in the workforce since Devin started kindergarten and although we weren't visibly rich by the world's standards, financially; our net-worth continued to accumulate.

We were still maintaining our own agenda though and not God's preordained purpose for our lives and were nowhere near reaching our personal goal of donating 10 percent of our income to help people experience and recognize the goodness of God. While we were always sure to pay into our equities first, we should have been paying God first. We tithed on a regular basis and were happy to do so but money was still very important to us, and because we were now a two-income household, we started to take advantage of that.

Randy and I cared little about being perceived as well-off and while I wouldn't have considered myself to be egotistical in any way, sadly, for some unknown reason, I felt compelled to improve our self-image and increase our material possessions. I upped the quality of our clothing and started to get my fingernails done professionally. We got a new vehicle—not used—for the very first time and my husband hired a landscaping company to babysit and nurture our grass. And while we don't feel we ever reck-lessly wasted our earnings, we were enjoying the very first hint of monetary freedom since the day we said "I do."

We were still keeping up with our investments, had significantly increased our deposits, and were grateful to God for watching over us and providing us with opportu-nities to grow, even when those opportunities for growth were masked as colossal waves in the turbulent ocean of life.

# OVERWHELMING ORDEALS

Chapter Nine

IN 2004, WE ENCOUNTERED A LEGAL COMPLICATION AND HAD to hire a lawyer. That's when Randy and I really began to panic about money. We didn't place our trust in God and insisted on handling everything ourselves. Fervent prayers were sent up to Jesus in Heaven, but in retrospect, I know we weren't asking for the right thing.

We were on an emotional and financial roller coaster and couldn't seem to find any way to get off. The more we fretted, the worse we felt. We couldn't wrap our minds around why our prayers weren't being answered and God seemed to be so silent and withdrawn.

Randy and I had already travelled down some challenging roads in our past but this one appeared to be headed toward a cliff. We were flat-out ignoring our Father's Word that says instead of worrying, we needed to have faith in

Him to receive the peace we were so desperately searching for. We were riddled with anxiety, carrying our heavy burden ourselves, and in the midst of a very significant object lesson about making God the top priority in our lives.

At the end of our court case, a registered letter arrived in the mail from our lawyer stating our balance owing was $50,000 and the deadline was in two weeks! All the blood in my body rushed to my head, my heart threatened to detonate inside my chest, and the light in my soul was promptly extinguished. Randy's mind reeled; he hung his head in defeat and started to cry. Our emergency fund didn't come close to covering the bill, we were completely overwhelmed and heavy stress commandeered every cell in our bodies.

We kept begging God to help us and then in the same breath arrogantly told Him what He ought to do to fix our dilemma. Even after we told Jesus what we needed, we were determined to deal with everything ourselves and didn't give God a chance to work. We didn't relinquish our fears to God, were not devoted or trusting, and attempted to give God instructions on how to oversee His jurisdiction. Our Bible tells us Jesus said, *"Come to me, all of you who are weary and carry heavy burdens, and I will give you rest"*

(Matthew 11:28) while Peter urged us to *"Give all your worries and cares to God, for he cares about you"* (1 Peter 5:7).

A treasured message from our Father was being taught to us and as much as we were hurting in the moment, we now feel blessed by our experience. Paul said, *"Always be joyful. Never stop praying. Be thankful in all circumstances, for this is God's will for you who belong to Christ Jesus"* (1 Thessalonians 5:16-18).

At that point in time, Randy and I certainly weren't thankful or joyful and were dreadfully failing at being in charge of our own lives. Of course, we weren't bad people and weren't breaking any laws, but like much of humanity, we were egotistical, selfish and self-centred, only caring about our wants, our motivations, and ourselves. Our marriage was based on putting the kids first, each other second, and God third. I can only imagine how dejected God must have felt to watch His beloved children in such an intense crisis and not have our permission to speak His words of wisdom, love, and encouragement into our pitiful, jittery hearts.

Even after all we'd been through up to that moment, we still hadn't come to the realization God was overseeing everything. God always hears our prayers, I am convinced of that, but I now know some of my prayers were shame-fully resentful. Even though I'd been going to church for many years I was missing many crucial points in the Bible; adopting the warm and fuzzy verses and ignoring the rest. Although I was pleased with my spiritual growth up until that point, I knew I still had a long way to go.

My walk with God has been a lengthy and tumultuous expedition. I frequently traveled beside God, basking in His wisdom, but more often than not, I stubbornly stomped up ahead of Him, trying to reach our destination first so I could be both the supervisor and CEO of our assignment.

I'm privileged to say I'm continually growing with God. My life today is so very different than it was even a few years ago. Not easier by any means, just better, more fulfilling, and more peaceful because I have a personal con-nection with Him and our relationship continues to evolve and mature every day. I put *all* my faith and assurance in Him and deeply regret wasting so many years not doing it sooner as it would have better equipped me for the mad-dening miseries that just kept on coming.

# CONTINUED CHAOS

Chapter Ten

SHORTLY AFTER TAKING OUT A BANK LOAN TO COVER OUR legal fees, Randy got informed we were moving, again. We did a few renovations, staged our home, and put it up for sale. The housing market was very slow that spring and once again, the distress set in. Will our house sell in time? What if it doesn't? Should we buy or rent at the other end?

Instead of calmly praying for guidance and relying on God to direct our situation, we foolishly held up our hands again and told Him "we've got this!" An offer came in. Acquaintances from our church had done a walk-through, loved what they saw, and said it was ideal for them. They put in an offer—a hint lower than we would have liked—but as a goodwill gesture, we accepted it. Yay! We were thrilled our house was unofficially sold.

We started scouting out places in the area we were moving to and it only took a few hours to find the perfect one. It was a little over the top of our budget and the couple were fairly firm on their price, but the layout and location paled in comparison to any other that we'd seen. We set our sights on that specific house and stopped the real estate search.

The sellers expected a closing date eight weeks earlier than we were able to move, but we decided to bite the bullet and pay the extra two months' mortgage just so we could own that incredible four-bedroom bungalow. The yard backed onto an enchanting, ankle-deep creek and we could picture our kids hanging out there and having the best summer of their lives. We made an offer and it was approved. Life was so good! After all the trouble, stress, and frustration we'd had over the court case, we were excited something was finally going right.

In retrospect, I guess we should have waited until the deal went through on the house we were living in before taking the next step. In retrospect, I guess we should have prayed over the transaction and submitted our desires to God (instead of ignoring Him) before entering into any commitments. In retrospect, I guess, no, I *know* we should have put God first in every area of our lives and asked Him for His advice and support. We should have heeded this verse: *"Seek his will in all you do, and he will show you which path to take"* (Proverbs 3:6).

Randy and I were not doing that, at all. We were only putting God first when it suited us and when things weren't going our way. I professed to be a Christian but basically only called out to God when I needed something. Sadly, I was more of a Sunday-morning-only Christian and my mate was just along for the ride.

Unfortunately, there was a complication with the offer on the house we were living in and the deal fell through. The buyers had changed their minds and went in a different direction. We were utterly devastated. We'd already lowered our number below our intention and were hysterical about the prospective profit loss. The move date was less than two months away and our home wasn't even sold. We were beyond angry, we were furious!

Our property didn't sell before our move and even though we'd just taken out a huge loan to pay our legal fees, we ended up having to borrow another $50,000 to cover the difference in the prices of the houses and our impending double-mortgage. The vile "For Sale'" sign stood crudely on the lawn as the moving company loaded our furniture onto the truck. We wearily settled into our new address with the headache of our old home refusing to leave the forefront of our thoughts.

The summer heat was replaced by the cool fall breeze. The snow arrived and we still owned—and were paying for—two dwellings. Randy and I were carrying a bitterness that had us spiraling in a vortex of negative emotion and we couldn't understand what we'd done wrong to be subjected to this perceived absence of God's presence. Where was He? Wasn't He watching what was happening to us? Didn't He care we were now down almost $100,000? Why wasn't He helping us?

For seven months, my husband and I carried both residences while desperately pleading to God for help. We were shamelessly blind to our faults and weren't even remotely close to seeing the error in our ways. Tempers were high, sleep was lost, and we were holding onto our resentment with a vice-like grip. The only thing on our minds was our stupid former house and the probability we were going to lose even more money if we had to drop the price again.

Money, money, money. Our priorities, which seemed so vital in the crux of that moment, were completely off base. We were so obsessed and consumed by our drama that we ran to our pastor for guidance. We explained our heavy sense of frustration, our unyielding anger, and our monetary defeat. Looking back, I can't believe we reacted in such an unbecoming manner and can only imagine how self-absorbed we must have seemed.

Randy and I were in the midst of a lesson in common sense and didn't even know it. God was chipping away at His beloved stones, attempting to round out a few uneven edges but it was a torturous process as we were still unwittingly determined to put our assets and investments at the top of our agenda.

That's how life lessons work. It takes time, lots of time, for character and integrity to develop. God was moulding and shaping us to become the joyously generous people we are today and we should have known He loves us and allows what's best in order for us to become the people we were designed to be. We had to endure some mind-bending and exceedingly difficult trials in order to see the blessings and light in our obstacles.

We got first-hand knowledge and insight in the application of the Lord's Prayer where it requires us to "forgive those who trespass against us." We were holding a ridiculous grudge against a couple who didn't deserve it and it definitely wasn't easy but we started praying for calmness in our hearts, worked diligently on our negative attitudes, and began living in a presence of forgiveness and leniency.

Choosing to forgive can never change the past, but it will change your future. Holding onto anger and resentment poisons your soul. By forgiving someone, you are actually setting yourself free from the unrelenting chains of hatred and your self-governed prison. The road of unforgiveness is straight and easy while the complex path to forgiveness takes guts, determination, and a desire to escape your own enslavement and soar to new heights of serenity.

We thanked God for the strength He imparted in us and the grace He'd granted us and our old house eventually sold.

Through the Holy Spirit's gentle whispers and finding rest in God's arms, Randy and I developed a powerful sense of peace. While the chaos was hard to undergo at the time, we're eternally indebted to the fellow church members who were slated to buy our home for representing such an integral part of our refinement process and helping us to mature into people God can truly be proud of.

We're not anywhere close to being fully polished yet, but the state of raw stone we were in many years ago seems like such a distant memory. Throughout that process, Randy and I continued on our journey as God's children, drawing nearer and closer to Him each day. We learned not to be optimistic because of what we felt, but because of what we knew about God. He turned our messes into messages and our tests into a testimony. He loves us. He is able. He is good!

# BREAKING
# EVEN

Chapter Eleven

I HAVE ALWAYS LIVED BY THE OLD ADAGE; "IT'S NEVER ABOUT how much money you make, it's always about how much money you spend." Consumers buy things they think will make them happy and then do nothing but resent their bills in the aftermath. Randy and I are relieved we haven't accumulated any unnecessary debt over the years as we have both witnessed the negative impact it can have on one's mental health and the seismic fractures it generates in the nuclear family.

Randy and I have always planned for the future together and I'm still grateful God united our like-mindedness in marriage almost three decades ago. While we weren't entirely successful, we worked hard on not succumbing to the pressure of always yearning for bigger and better. We now see God wants us to enjoy the blessings

He provides, and are in the process of implementing that foreign concept.

Once God gifted us with another increase in income, we added more to our children's education accounts, often doubled our mortgage payments, and welcomed the sprinkle of leftover dollars to use for ourselves. Our tithing was getting close to our goal but we still weren't fully relying on God with our finances. While we don't feel we were ever wasteful, there've been a few instances over the years when we figured out, after the fact, that our spending left a lot to be desired.

For many years, my sweetheart and I went to a local casino to celebrate our birthdays and anniversary. Randy would play his poker tables and I would play my slots, then we'd share a delicious meal and stay the night at a nearby hotel. We never gambled more than we'd allotted (usually $100 for Randy and $50 for me) and we always looked forward to our next visit.

Although I'd often considered that God wouldn't appreciate us acting so flippant with our funds, we rationalized our evening by claiming it as a jovial and entertaining holiday. Goodness, it wasn't like we were high rollers and breaking the bank. Even though I'd always felt a little icky for losing my $50, my poker master ordinarily came out ahead so we would typically break even. That was fun for a while…until it wasn't.

There came a time when I started to get a bad feeling about going to the casino before I even went. That's called conviction. I knew God had been blessing us financially, but was He pleased with what we were doing with our money or was He disappointed? What was our point in trying to win big? Didn't we trust God enough to sustain our every need? With every drop of a cool, shiny token and every eager tug on the one-armed-bandit, He was nudging me toward the conclusion our resources could definitely be used in a more beneficial manner.

I can honestly say, in our dozens of escapades at the casino over the years, I've never won the pot of gold at the end of the rainbow and rarely broke even. I sat in cushy casino chairs and spin after spin, pull after arm-numbing pull, wished and hoped and prayed that the bells and whistles would blast in my favour, and always left disappointed. Was I just unlucky or was it possible God was trying to tell me something?

I won't forget the day it happened. The revelation slipped into my mind and twitched around like an untold secret. I finally realized our money is not *our* money! Our bank account had been provided to us by God through the generous opportunities He had orchestrated for us. I shared my thoughts with Randy, we prayed together, and our outlook changed. We agreed to stop tormenting ourselves with our independence and hand God our full allegiance in every aspect of our lives. God was God for a reason and we put our complete trust in His goodness and love.

If we ever go to a casino again it will assuredly be a rare occurrence and our reason for going would not include a desire to be millionaires. I had just finished wrapping my head around the reality that God would truly supply all my needs when something bizarre happened.

In a way I wouldn't have to work for, a chance to fill our bank account arrived out of nowhere and threw me for a total loop. We were already praying for wisdom before making donations, supporting local Christian businesses as often as we could, aiding foreign faith-based organizations that were doing hands-on work for God, and consistently using God's Word as a foundation for our expenditures, so it was hard for me to tell if this prospect was going to be a benefit or a burden.

# STRIKE IT RICH

Chapter Twelve

TODAY'S CULTURE ALWAYS SEEMS TO CRAVE MORE. A BIGGER castle, a nicer ride, recreational equipment, and to win the lottery often top people's most wanted lists. Back when the kids were in diapers and we were concerned about making ends meet, we'd buy a handful of lottery tickets now and again when the jackpot was big. But that was years ago.

As a couple, we've never really felt we were missing out on anything (even when I had to borrow change from the babes to buy milk), but once in a while when the prize would have been enough to last a lifetime, we assumed it would be nice to be rich. But sometimes we want things we don't need, sometimes we need things we don't want, and sometimes we want things we already have.

People in my inner circle got a good giggle when I received a scratch lottery ticket in my birthday card one time.

It was shortly after we had stopped visiting the casino and I hadn't purchased a lotto in many years. I gingerly held the ticket in my hand like it was toxic waste and blankly stared at it like I didn't know what it was. In my commitment to God, I already knew *"Wherever your treasure is, there the desires of your heart will also be"* (Matthew 6:21) and *"For the love of money is the root of all kinds of evil. And some people, craving money, have wandered from the true faith and pierced themselves with many sorrows"* (1 Timothy 6:10).

My desire to be wealthy had already dissipated and my core beliefs were thrown into complete turmoil. What was I supposed to do with this $3 ticket? Did God want me to scratch it? Would He be upset if I did? What would I buy if I won the jackpot?

My conscience was wrestling with what I presumed was a salvation-altering choice. You would have thought it was a life or death predicament with the amount of stock and emotion I was putting into it. I prayed about it, phoned my mother, texted a Christian friend, and tried to determine WWPD (what would my pastor do)? Was it God's plan for me to be filthy-rich? What would I do if I scratched and won a million bucks?

As we already dwelled in a state of thankfulness and didn't need anything materially, would I be able to bless others in a bigger way? Was I being tempted? Most didn't see what the big deal was and felt I should just scratch it. I stuck it in the fruit bowl and every morning its glittery little squares would gleam in the sunlight. If I scratched it I believed I would win big and then have an even greater predicament on my hands with what to do with my new-found riches.

After an agonizing week of the ticket peeking out at me from behind the bananas, I decided to give in and scratch it. I sat down in my dead-quiet kitchen with a brand-new penny and methodically removed each tiny square, fantasizing about my upcoming windfall of prosperity.

I got down to the wire, with only one silver dot to go to become the lucky winner of $10,000 and thought; "this is it, this is so awesome, what am I going to do with my unexpected fortune?" With shaking hands, I scratched the last square—only to reveal...I hadn't won! Seriously? All that hype for nothing? The phone calls and heart-to-hearts for nothing? Oh my.

Did I learn a lesson that day? Of course I did. Does God have a sense of humour? I imagine He does. This conundrum over the ticket really had nothing to do with the ticket. It was about going to God when we're not sure what to do. I know God was proud of me for actually taking the time to wrestle with my indecisiveness over whether to scratch or not, and He loved seeing me question others to solicit their spiritual guidance.

I'd reached a period in my life, through God's love, patience, and mercy, that if I would have won the jackpot, there wouldn't have been one thing I'd have wanted to buy for myself and would only wonder who I would get to treat first. Resting in God, I knew He would provide all the things money couldn't buy: the welfare of our children, the solidness of our marriage, our future in Heaven, and His never-ending love for me. I know it's tough to envision how one silly ticket triggered such a giant quandary, but I can say, undeniably, I'd have donated all my imaginary winnings to God's work. For that reason alone I'm glad I got that ticket as it brought me even closer to God's purpose and design for my life.

Gradually, as our walk with God intensified, it dawned on us we were already rich. Randy and I were economically stable—including our double-mortgage and astronomical lawyer loan—had a great marriage (not without its ups and downs), three amazing kids, a nice place to live, steady and rewarding jobs, positive relationships with extended family, and were cherished children of our Father in Heaven. The things that were essential to us in the past just didn't hold the same luster and significance they used to and we became content to thoroughly enjoy the many gifts that God had already given us.

In the past few years, public opinion has become an unfortunate frontrunner in determining our self-worth, especially when it relates to social media. Many have a look-at-me attitude, desperate to feel deserving of a stranger's praise, rack up "likes" in the triple-digits, be considered a person of high esteem, get as many followers on Instagram as possible, and soar into an atmosphere of fame, fortune, and popularity.

People compare the reality of their own story to someone else's highlight reel—and it does nothing but dampen their mood, depress their joy, and bring them down. Screen time should improve our life, not be our life.

It was a gratifying feeling when we finally grasped that the only person we should be trying to please is God. Our entire outlook changed. When Randy and I began running everything by God first before making hasty decisions, even conversing with Him about normal day-to-day events, we gained a noticeable shift in our happiness. When we started living for God instead of living for ourselves, we truly started to live.

As a couple, Randy and I have happily donated to many charities and non-profit organizations over the years and we've always considered ourselves voluntarily generous, but a while back, we took a thorough account of where our contributions were actually going. We sought to participate more in foundations that were direct extensions of God's own hand; the lost, the broken, and the less fortunate were silently calling out to us to be their instruments of hope and our hearts were hungry to help them. But because we were already supporting so many charities, something had to give.

We did a total reassessment by investigating our endowments more thoroughly and researching new worthwhile groups, subtracting some and adding others. We finalized our list and were pleased with the result as it then represented our relationship with God and our dedication and commitment to Him. Our family is privileged to share the love of Jesus Christ through our finances and are confident that in doing so, God acknowledges our devotion and will honour us in return. We believe:

*Give, and you will receive. Your gift will return to you in full—pressed down, shaken together to make room for more, running over, and poured into your lap. The amount you give will determine the amount you get back.*
—Luke 6:38

When Randy and I truly started blessing others, we found *we* were truly blessed. We started to appreciate the smaller things in life. Our desire for more material possessions disappeared and we became content with what we had. We watched intently as God created a masterpiece from our brokenness and were amazed by His unending grace and forgiveness. We had collectively made many mistakes over the years but gradually the depth of God's love for us became more evident than ever.

# ONE MAN'S TRASH...

Chapter Thirteen

I WAS VINTAGE BEFORE VINTAGE WAS EVEN COOL. THRIFT STORE finds are currently all the rage and "thrift therapy" has become an actual term. Trendy consignment shops are popping up all around the cities and naturally my daughter and I still utilize a personal account at one of them.

Right after Luc was born, we welcomed a small bag of hand-me-downs from our nephew containing the most charming pair of Nike running slippers. I balk at the notion of calling them shoes as infants aren't physically capable of actually walking anywhere. Our baby boy had received a number of new outfits as gifts and we were captivated by these cool little Nikes that matched everything perfectly. We couldn't afford shoes like that for our baby and were elated to put such an upscale item on him.

Our prenatal class had a meet-and-greet reunion when all the babies were about six months old. Most families we'd laboured with in the class were well-to-do and I can remember feeling ridiculously dignified to display these tiny Nikes on Luc so we'd fit in better and wouldn't look so low-income. Upon reflection, I'm mortified for thinking that way over something so superficial, for *"... The Lord doesn't see things the way you see them. People judge by outward appearance, but the Lord looks at the heart"* (1 Samuel 16:7).

Were we perceived as poor by the other parents in the class? Maybe. Should it have mattered what they thought? Of course not. But I was immature and foolish and honestly imagined a pair of baby slippers would improve the illusion of our economic stability and boost our self-image.

In those days, we had no concept of the awe-inspiring connection between God and finances, including blessings and tithings. I'd been going to church since primary school but the lessons acquired as children are very different from the teachings we receive as adults. Our experiences mould and shape us into the people we become and should all be considered as either something to improve upon or to not do again. Thankfully, those sweet Nikes introduced me to the wonderful realm of second-hand shopping, a practice I still happily engage in today.

While Luc, Jes, and Dev never had a huge collection of clothes, they certainly had enough to get by as I never saw the need to have drawers and closets overflowing with unworn apparel. They would generally get a few new outfits for Christmas and birthdays (as well as exciting toys and board games) and always got cute matching outfits for our annual holiday photo. Throughout the remainder of the year, I'd hunt for amazing finds at all available second-hand stores and it didn't matter if I found something three sizes too big, if I thought the kids would like it and wear it, I would buy it and store it in my giant surplus of storage totes.

One time however, my smart storage strategy got me into unforeseen trouble. Before we had access to the Internet and the entire universe was obsessed with online shopping, like every other person in civilization with a mailbox, I got the Sears catalogues in the mail. Occasionally, a flyer tucked inside the catalogue would display super sell-off deals and one morning I noticed some very nice (read: expensive) boy's jeans on clearance for $12.99.

Randy and I discussed it and were sure these jeans would be a good investment in our boys' wardrobe so we bought six pairs in gradual sizing, three for each son. The boys were thrilled with their new jeans—and it wasn't even Christmas or their birthday—and I tucked the other pairs away for later.

In a flash, they outgrew the first pair and had to move up to the next size. As I rearranged our collection of too-big clothes, I sorted through the storage containers, brought out a couple of new-to-you items for the kids and took a few things out of their closets to be donated. I figured it wouldn't be long before the boys grew out of the second pair of brand-new jeans as well so I tucked the two remaining pairs in the top of their closet rather than back in the storage bin. And there they sat. For some odd reason, those dapper jeans didn't resurface again until we were moving and they were in there for so many seasons that I didn't even remember I had them.

As I pulled the crisp, dust-covered denim from the top closet shelf, I was dumbstruck. Where did these jeans come from? Whose were they? As the realization set in, I held the jeans open to gauge if they would still fit Luc or Jes. As the boys were practically the same size at the time, I got a bad feeling as I called them into the room. They didn't even have to try them on. I could tell just by looking that the cool jeans Randy and I'd had a serious, contemplative conversation over were no longer of use to us.

I know it may not have seemed like a tear-worthy moment to most, but I literally was sick to my stomach. The loss evoked a sense of failure in me, probably because I was always so attentive to our expenditures and this was a splurge we wouldn't have typically indulged in at a time when dollars were so tight. My level-headed hubby wasn't too concerned about the issue and felt we couldn't do anything about it so there was no use dwelling on it. Thank goodness he has always been the grounded one; that's never been one of my strengths!

Even though I didn't realize it back then, it was just another bend on the road of our pilgrimage with God. We knew of a fellow community member who had fallen on hard times and definitely required our two new pairs of jeans. We offered his wife the pants; she willingly accepted and was extremely grateful. Randy and I were honoured to show kindness to another couple in such a rewarding way and it led us directly onto the path of our predetermined, God-ordained ministry of sharing much of what we have with others who need it most.

The real reason I felt so queasy when the lost jeans turned up was because at that time I was still clueless about trusting God with our finances. I was relying on my own understanding and didn't embrace this wise scripture: *"Trust in the Lord with all your heart; do not depend on your own understanding"* (Proverbs 3:5).

Walking with God involves a lifetime of teachings, including years of His guidance and correction. He folds us in His loving arms and uses enlightening opportunities to enhance our lives. In the Psalms we read: *"He will cover you with his feathers. He will shelter you with his wings. His faithful promises are your armor and protection"* (Psalm 91:4).

Again, this was another event we can look back on now and see all the puzzle pieces fitting into place. We never cease to be amazed at the intricacy of God's approach and how He instils characteristics in us He will later use to help those around us. Because of the inexplicable joy Randy and I got a taste of many years ago when we shared our jeans with the other family, we are still paying it forward (usually anonymously) in unique and fun ways.

Hidden heroes influence God's kingdom one heart at a time. Ministry shouldn't be glory-filled. The quiet sense of fulfilling God's plan without any public fame or praise has been one of the most enriching and focus-changing acts we've ever participated in, and each month we eagerly anticipate seeing where our prayers will lead us in serving others through the love of Jesus Christ.

# THE MIDDLE YEARS

Chapter Fourteen

OH, THE MIDDLE YEARS. EVERY TRIBE SINCE THE DAWN OF history has endured the middle years. A few do it with finesse; others like us lumber along blindly, praying for the best and five minutes of parenting peace.

Luc, Jesse, and Devin engaged in many activities over the years. Not too many, just enough to keep them occupied and out of mischief. Every now and then we'd find the demands of the ever-popular winter hockey to be a bit much as all three children participated in and loved the camaraderie of the team sport. Randy and I got personally involved as coach and team manager and as a family we visited the arena four or five times per week, six months every year, for sixteen years! Oh my. Yes, once in a while it got a tad overwhelming and physically and mentally draining, but all in all, it was time well spent.

Early on in our hockey life, my children became wistfully aware of the expected after-hockey treat. Our kids were disappointed to discover that even though we had never really been big on junk food, many other families were. When we first signed up for hockey, we were barely scraping by after budgeting for the registration and equipment, and my honey and I set the precedent right away that we weren't going to be squandering what few loonies we had on arena food; not for the kids, and not for ourselves either.

As there were many children on the team whose parents were fairly well-off (remember the Real Housewives of Moms and Tots?), it was a popular topic in the dressing room after practice for them to declare what they were all getting at the canteen.

After explaining to our kids our brood wasn't going to be taking part in the lure of the concession stand and they could have a snack when they got home, Randy and I sustained the unnerving pain of looking into all their sad puppy-dog eyes and standing firm.

As the children got older and could comprehend the concept of money better, I constructed a small chart and totalled up the amount we were saving by not being slaves to the unhealthy goodies at the food booth. When they could see how much we were saving for three children, numerous times a week for a whole year, they begrudgingly accepted our viewpoint.

To be clear, it's not like we were ogres and the kids never got an after-hockey indulgence. At every tournament—and there were many—they would each get $10 to buy whatever tickled their fancy and because it didn't happen every day, it was considered a treat; an occasional splurge that made it special, and their dad and I felt good about instilling those important principles in our children.

At the end of every hockey season, we took what we had saved on junky snacks and rewarded our kids with fun-filled mini-vacations and knew they were a much better use of our hard-earned wages. Throughout the middle years, I, like most parents, often second-guessed our child-rearing skills and found myself questioning our decisions. However, it was always essential to us and nonnegotiable to raise our daughter and sons with a strong, sensible Christian foundation and the crucial concept that your cash going out should never exceed your cash coming in.

We never had an official discussion with our children about receiving an allowance, but it obviously came to a head one day when one of the kids stomped in to the kitchen, hands on their hips, and sassily asked why they didn't get paid for their chores like all their friends did. Randy and I often made it possible for our children to earn money for doing bigger tasks such as cutting the grass and piling firewood, but we always agreed our kids wouldn't pocket payment for sharing in the housework that they had helped to create.

It was a rocky road for us. Their father and I explained repeatedly—in some cases, heatedly—that our party of five, who lived cohesively under the same roof, should work together as a unit; they wouldn't be paid to wash dishes they ate off, to put away laundry they wore, and make the beds they slept in.

Although we successfully stood our ground over the years, it took the kids ages to stop asking and I don't think they ever really picked up on the method to our madness. Time will tell though and we're comically curious to see if our future grandkids will end up getting paid to fold their own socks.

Now seems like the perfect chance to set the record straight, in case it might be perceived my soulmate and I were browbeating jail wardens who didn't buy their children food and enlisted them in slave labour; Lucas, Jesse, and Devin Leighton were *privileged* children. Yes, they wore second-hand clothes up until high-school, didn't routinely get candy at the arena, and had to wash the family dishes—for free—but before we even had kids, Randy and I made a commitment to each other to be involved parents and we thank God we've always been the close knit bunch we still are today.

We've spent almost every possible waking moment with our children, taking them on dozens of vacations, playing board games on rainy days, having backpacking trips and movie theatre nights, experiencing cultural and historical excursions, beach afternoons, and unforgettable life adventures.

It must have been traumatic for our children to only have $1 for the summer camp tuck shop instead of $5 like their sunburnt friends, but we believed, without reservation, we were implanting immeasurable wisdom and were diligently praying some of those ideals stuck.

If not getting a bag of gummy bears at the arena and not receiving a weekly allowance didn't add enough insult to injury for our kids, over the years we've always taken a lunch in the car. As a military family, we've endured countless hours travelling to and from relatives and very early on, even for ourselves, Randy and I got in the habit of bringing our own meals and snacks, for both savings and convenience.

The kids still joke today about our on-the-road back-seat feasts, but now as young adults, are fully aware of the outrageous cost of restaurant food and the daylight we'd have wasted getting to the cottage while waiting for some-one to cook our food.

Because we enjoyed many activities together—also known to our kids as "Good Family Fun"—and went on an outing, or to an event, a couple of times every month for over 20 years, we've had to eat hundreds of meals away from home. Originally, we brought our own food because we didn't have the extra money to purchase restaurant fare, but over time, when we actually had a little cash for frivolity, we could never justify dropping a hundred dollars on one meal when we knew I could pay the same amount at the grocery store and feed our whole clan for an entire week!

# EATING OUT

Chapter Fifteen

I VIVIDLY REMEMBER THE DAY I FELT GOD'S UNMISTAKABLE love touch my heart more than it ever had before. My guy was working out of town for a month so in order for us not to be apart so long, we splurged on a family campsite right in the centre of the city. We ate dinner together every night and roasted marshmallows over the fire and during the day I did my best to entertain the kids. Unfortunately, the campground was attached to an amusement park and I had to explain to our three sweet children we legitimately didn't have the money to spend on rides and games.

Truthfully, not having the ability to take advantage of the close proximity to the amusement rides crushed my self-esteem and made me feel like a terrible mother. I really wanted to do something exciting with our kids while Randy was at work during the day but stay-at-home mommies rarely have an overload of leftover change in their wallets. The look of longing in their eyes as they heard the squeals of delight from other children on the mini-coaster was more than I could bear and I cried myself to sleep that night in my husband's arms.

A few days into the trip, to try to make up for our inability to afford the rides, I considered taking the kids to McDonald's PlayPlace for the afternoon. I knew they'd plead for Happy Meals but we didn't have the additional $20 for a restaurant lunch as the summer fees at the waterfront park were significantly more than we were accustomed to for camping.

The next day, as I was out for a brief, peaceful, mommy-only-time-jog before Daddy left for work, my world turned upside down. There, right in the middle of the gigantic vacant parking lot, at 6 a.m., on an unseasonably cool and rainy August morning, laid a $20 bill! As I stared at the money, the exact amount we would need to cover lunch for four at McDonald's, I was completely shaken to my core. A jumble of thoughts raced around in my head and I stood there, shell shocked and overcome with emotion.

While the general public swears by karma and coincidences, Christians firmly believe in "God-sidences." God heard the desire of my heart and knew I would run in that exact area of the massive empty parking lot that normally held hundreds and hundreds of cars. I looked around to see if there was someone I could return the money to, but at that early hour on God's grey morning, there was not a single soul in sight. Standing there in the soft drizzle, I was in absolute awe of God's tremendous power and did not doubt for one second He planted that gift on my path. My legs and hands were shaking as I slowly bent to retrieve the soggy bill.

I was very quiet that day as the torrents of rain streamed down the windows of the restaurant. I unconsciously spun back and forth in the rock-hard McDonald's chair as I watched the eyes of my babies light up at the toy in their Happy Meal. An unspeakable joy flowed down my cheeks as they ate their French fries and played in the ball pit. God couldn't have chosen a better day for us to play indoors.

I knew I'd had a Godly experience and it still brings tears to my eyes when I think of it. I was deeply moved that God recognized such a simple wish and it greatly enhanced my faith to know I hadn't even prayed for it. God physically touched my spirit and awakened me to a more intimate relationship with Him. While I'm still blown away by the many ways He uses to get our attention, I've often wondered how many more times God tries to catch our eye and we're just too preoccupied to notice.

Throughout the busyness of the middle years, we typically saved restaurants for special occasions but made sure to take advantage of the "kids eat free nights" whenever we could. That is until the kids got to be too old to be "kids" and we switched to a fast food restaurant that quickly became our go-to with its yummy and affordable $1.39 value menu. The kids always got to pick a few delicious things and our entire group could eat for about $25. As the children got older and the value options weren't enough to fill their growing bellies, we found a local diner that served insanely enormous portions for ridiculously reasonable prices and that became our favourite spot for the celebratory moments in our lives.

During our 16 years of hockey tournaments with hotel stays, I became very adept at preparing enough food for all our meals and making it fit into one cooler. Our hockey organization encouraged everyone to bring food from home as opposed to wasting our life savings on restaurants, and I was particularly grateful for that.

I'd bake, freeze, and wrap banana muffins, pour Texas chili into sealable plastic bags for transport, and cut loads of veggie sticks to eat with our ready-to-heat lasagne. Also included were the ingredients for a huge chicken Caesar salad and a large mixing bowl, tongs, and tortilla wraps for a wholesome meal. I often carried our sandwich maker to make grilled cheese sandwiches and sometimes even brought the crockpot for mouth-watering pulled pork. Easy peasy.

It delighted me most other families on the team were on the same wavelength as us about avoiding dining out, so we didn't feel like we were missing out on team suppers. We'd hold potluck dinners in the hotel breakfast area for the entire team and everyone would participate with their hotel-cooked eats.

Please, don't misunderstand. Food preparation takes forever and a day and lots and lots of patience. Preparing enough food for our whole gang for a three-day weekend, once or twice a month for all those years, while working full-time and running a busy household, was stressful and exhausting for me. I'd occasionally enlist Randy or the children to lend a hand, but with them working or in school, most of the arrangements fell on my shoulders.

However, my supermom efforts paid off in the end with the knowledge I'd personally save us thousands of dollars by organizing ahead and preparing nutritious and inexpensive meals on the go. At the end of each tournament, we'd usually be out of food—and energy—and stop for a fresh burger on our way home; a relief to not have to cook and inwardly rewarding because my resourceful meal planning over the years had saved us a tonne of cash!

# THE REASON
# FOR THE SEASON

Chapter Sixteen

FROM THE BEGINNING, WE'VE MADE IT A PRIORITY NOT TO PUT Santa before our Saviour. I regret not taking the opportunity with our young children to celebrate the birth of baby Jesus with a mini-party for Him. I would have included "It's a Boy" balloons and a decorated chocolate cake, but it's possible the two thousand or so candles might have been a fire hazard!

Even though it's something I didn't get to do with my own kids, I fully intend on belting out Happy Birthday to Jesus in unison with all my wee grandkids someday. I can't wait.

When Luc, Jes, and Dev were small, we began every Christmas morning with the story of Jesus's birth. Mary and Joseph, shepherds and wise men, a donkey and a lowly manger held a place of honour with us and we wanted to ensure we paid tribute to them before diving into presents. It was critical to Randy and I that they knew the reason for the season—and it had absolutely nothing to do with them being bad or good.

Like a pirate, I was forever on a quest for perfect treasures for our kids. I always picked out gifts I was sure they'd love, without me having to break the bank. While many don't even entertain the idea of Christmas shopping until after Thanksgiving, I diligently scouted for amazing finds at discount and sale prices all year round. Since Randy was away on training at least half of the year, I always did the shopping, but we were in complete agreement we were under no obligation to squander thousands of dollars to give our children a fulfilling and joyous Christmas.

When the kids were young, and thankfully didn't understand the value of money, Randy and I, because of our socioeconomic status, spent a little less on Christmas than the rest of society. While our children always received many useful and entertaining treats from grandparents and aunts and uncles, their mom, dad, and Santa, just bought what they could affordably manage. I'm so glad I never had to stand outside in the biting December air with dozens of other frenzied customers, impatiently waiting for the store doors to open so I could race inside and greedily yank the toy-of-the-year out of another consumer's hand. And while our kids always got great gifts, we mostly concentrated on our two weeks off together by visiting the toboggan hill, going ice skating, baking sugar cookies, listening to our Barney Christmas CD, and playing festive board games. We loved the holidays!

Christmas is a time when much of the public gets caught in the hype of keeping up with the latest trend. Companies come out with fantastic marketing campaigns that brainwash everyone and convince them they need more…more of everything. Sadly, many buy into that ploy, recklessly purchasing a bunch of stuff they can't afford, and seeming confused to find themselves in immense debt at the end of the season. Extravagance and debt are a toxic combination that cause unnecessary anxiety and torment, and ultimately increase familial stress to an uncontrollable level.

Moms and dads figure out they're behind on their bills due to lavishing their sons and daughters with a host of things they didn't require. When they don't put their confidence in God to provide all their needs, money becomes their primary focus and all other important ideals slip away. I'm reminded: *"No one can serve two masters. For you will hate one and love the other; you will be devoted to one and despise the other. You cannot serve God and be enslaved to money"* (Matthew 6:24).

It baffles me families who are in debt frequently dream of winning the lottery. They already have so many material possessions and can't pay the bills they have, yet they continue to pine for more, more, more.

Twenty-nine years into marriage, Randy and I still share the same principles of fiscal fitness we did as newlyweds, but gratefully our views have graduated from being thoroughly self-centred to fully Christ-centred. We know God is in dominion over our net worth and will assist us with all we need. We accept and have faith in His ability to oversee our purchases.

As a couple, we've never given in to advertising, only bought what we could afford, and been successful in explaining to our children the dangers of letting your savings drop into the red.

Many years ago, in a period when Randy and I were especially wary of wasting any of the meagre income we had, I became witness to a calamity in the making. A neighbour and I were discussing holiday shopping and she giddily revealed how much she adored Christmastime. She was over the moon about buying presents for her kids. This woman and her partner both had good-paying professions and lived accordingly. They never bothered with buying things on sale, had a huge house with a pool and two flashy vehicles, and bought whatever they wanted whenever they wanted it. The notion of ever having to suffer from a lack of expendable cash flow never crossed their minds.

She energetically proceeded to tell me about all the gifts she'd bought for her three children—what was going in their stockings, what Santa was bringing them, and what they were getting for themselves. I was flabbergasted! She had shelled out thousands of dollars and spent more for her children's stockings than I had spent on stockings, Santa, and Mommy and Daddy combined! I was embarrassed and ashamed because I meticulously guarded our limits and only paid a few hundred dollars for presents for our three kids.

For a brief minute, the world caught up with me and I felt like a heel for not buying more. Then, I came to my senses. I used it as a teaching moment for our roundtable dinner that night and replayed my conversation with our neighbour to Randy and the kids. I didn't leave anything out, especially not the amount I figured she'd blown through, and my humiliation of not having the ability or willingness to do the same.

We had a wonderful discussion with our children about how they have a duty to save for upcoming necessities, what it meant to be content, the positive influence money can have on the underprivileged, the importance of not exceeding your limits, and how we celebrate Christ's birth first and foremost and not the number or monetary worth of presents we get.

Randy and I don't feel Luc, Jes, or Dev were ever deprived in any way and honestly hope we helped them mature into appreciative adults by sharing our wisdom and intuition all throughout their childhood.

Years later, I happened to bump into that same woman who'd senselessly wasted so much money on Christmas. Her first child was heading off to college and she was flat out distraught because the government had only supplied them with a small loan to cover their son's expenses. The loan offer was based on the combined income of the parents and because their income was still high, they didn't even get enough to cover the tuition and books, let alone the accommodation fees.

She tearfully explained to me they were heavily in debt and didn't know how they were going to come up with the money to send their son to college. I sincerely sympathized with her and lent her my listening ear as it pained me to see her in such distress. But that conversation also brought to light the self-satisfaction of knowing that Randy and I had successfully avoided conforming to the relentless demands of commercialism over the years and I silently patted myself on the back for my perseverance in saving whenever I could and always sticking to our budget.

# THRIFTY SPENDERS OR SPENDTHRIFTS?

Chapter Seventeen

OVER THE YEARS, THERE HAVE BEEN TIMES WE'VE SPENT BOTH a little too much and not nearly as much as we'd wanted to. For Devin's first birthday, we bought her a pail and shovel set for the sand box and a brightly coloured kick-ball. Both toys combined cost less than five dollars. Because we didn't have an overabundance of funds, three-year-old Lucas and two-year-old Jesse presumed a penny and a quarter held the same value, and gap-toothed Devin didn't know what she was missing. Randy and I were both satisfied and depressed by our purchase.

Looking back, we see we shouldn't have been disheartened at all. We bought what we could afford at a time when extra funds were practically nonexistent and we were instilling in our children to be thankful for all gifts, not just the ones that cost the most. Devin received numerous other birthday gifts from her grandparents, and Luc and Jes were thrilled Mommy said Devin's baby-faced smiles meant that she would love to share her new birthday toys with her brothers.

Christmas presents were sparse the year we were carrying our double-mortgage too. Our children didn't suffer by any means but we bought less than usual and thoroughly explained the reason why. They were understanding (or at least pretended to be) and seemed satisfied with their gifts. But on occasion over the years, we have made several extravagant purchases as well and it's obvious to us now those items we paid too much for were all an integral part of growing in wisdom.

A couple of years after our children were born, while we were still on one mediocre income, I needed an outfit to wear to a holiday function at Randy's work. As I'd delivered three babies in less than three years and still hadn't returned to my pre-pregnancy weight, I literally didn't have a thing to wear. I was aware the dress code necessitated something a little fancy and that was going to cost me plenty.

I flitted from store to store, wishing and hoping the right dress would just jump off the rack and onto my body. Twice I went to a tremendous amount of trouble to go shopping without my tots and twice I returned home empty-handed. Everything I tried on was too big or too small, too expensive or not expensive enough. I was frantic at the thought of not finding a dress and I was running out of time.

I was dying to find something suitable that fit into our budget but was failing miserably. Other than our anniversary, which we always tried to celebrate with a restaurant meal, Randy and I never had date nights and this no-kids-allowed party was very important to me and crucial for my mental health.

If this long-ago dress search was happening today, I'd ask Jesus in advance for guidance. I'd fold my hands, bow my head, and humbly ask that God direct me to the ideal dress, supply the additional funds to buy it, and be thankful for His presence in my life.

In those days, in which I was so desperate for a dress, I wasn't in the same in-depth relationship with God I am today. I didn't put God first, didn't pray for the perfect dress, and I certainly didn't know God already had it all under control. Chugging away like the Little-Engine-That-Could, all alone, I thought I could do it all myself, and discovered the hard way, it's impossible.

Many people appear to be so happy, living their lives without God, but appearances are so deceiving. They portray the impression they have it all in check, lucky to have good families, successful careers, many material possessions, and not a care in the world. And truthfully, they might even think everything is going great and they don't have any need for God.

But eventually, everyone needs Him. Recognizing it usually occurs during instances of great tragedy and sadly, some still refuse to turn to Him and keep trying to find a way to work it out on their own. They hire a life coach, placing all confidence and credence in their opinion, when the only manual they require is the Bible and the only instructor they should count on is God.

My life was very different before I started trusting God. It was filled with envy, pride, selfishness, and a frustrating emptiness that no matter what I tried couldn't be filled to satisfaction. It's not that Christians have different lives than those who don't rely on God. They suffer the same everyday challenges of chronic illness, job loss, raising teenagers, family estrangement, and the death of loved ones. While these complications are definitely not easy for God's children and they still undergo grief, universal stress, and pain, Christians are better equipped to face obstacles with God by their side, assured He knows them intimately, has plans for them to prosper, and loves them with His whole heart. We can experience true joy when we accept the limitations of our situation and depend on God to work through them and beyond.

I don't need to wonder if I would have been able to find an affordable outfit for the party sooner if I'd have left it up to God. He and I would have gone shopping together and together we'd have found a dress. On my third and final attempt, I bowed to the time constraint and cost of the outfit and bought a beautiful black gown. It was significantly more than I had aimed to pay and I sensed the sting of hot tears as I forked over my credit card. I'd always prided myself on not overspending but succumbed to the unrelenting pressure and immediately became concerned about how we'd cover the bill when it arrived.

Saying yes to the dress was the perfect enlightenment for me. It cost too much—which made me cherish it even more—but I was glad I recognized it. I also knew, one hundred percent for sure, I didn't want to do it again because I hated the anticipation of our impending credit card bill and that was an emotion I didn't care to feel on a regular basis.

# TRUST AND OBEY

Chapter Eighteen

TRUSTING GOD SHOULD BE AN EFFORTLESS AND SIMPLE PROCESS. As soon as our eyes flutter open in the morning, the world and our day can be filled with beauty and optimism because we know God is good and that everything works out for the benefit of those who love Him. How can the hurdles of life trip us into fear and unbelief when we know there is victory at the end of the race? Trusting God should be easy, but sometimes it's hard. We are so used to controlling our own lives that we slip up once in a while and allow doubt to fester in our minds. But the key point is to recognize that doubt, banish it from our thoughts, and continue running forward with a clear head and our goal in sight.

Ten years ago, our family had the chance to put all our financial dependence in God's hands. While that's an act we'd have aspired to achieve naturally, we were left with no choice but to trust God with every single fibre of our being. Thankfully, we'd already put our total assurance in God to watch over and provide for us when crisis struck. I was diagnosed with an incurable chronic illness and had to significantly cut my income.

I had no alternative but to reduce my employment from full-time to casual part-time. It was difficult for my gang as they transitioned from Mom being able to work, cook and clean, run the roads with hockey, and be at constant beck and call, to coping independently and fending for themselves; a concept that was mighty foreign to them. We still skillfully managed to make ends meet though by making some changes to our bills and investments but then, only two years later, another speed bump appeared out of nowhere that nearly sent us over the edge.

In order to avoid moving with the military again and keep our children in their hometown close to their grandparents, Randy had retired from the army four years prior. As he had retired at a stage in his career in which his pension was fairly small, he was beyond blessed to have secured a local position as a full-time military reservist. The income from Randy's pension coupled with his wage as a reservist was the approximate equivalent of what he'd been earning if he'd remained in the Canadian Forces full-time.

Then the annual, governmental federal budget was announced and implemented: all Canadian military personnel that were retired, collecting their pension, and working full-time in The Reserve Force, were being cut back to a part-time contract. That meant Randy. As he'd taken an early retirement and his pension amount was low, and I was only working casual hours and receiving a mediocre paycheque, we wouldn't be able to financially survive when my sweetheart's job was reduced to part-time. We had just built our dream home, which certainly wasn't cheap, and we still had three active and hungry teenagers living with us.

For a brief moment, our human natures took over and we started to fret. Then the Holy Spirit tenderly reminded us not to be nervous and everything was under control. We diligently prayed and vowed to leave it all in God's hands as Randy applied to get back into the full-time military. We agreed I would stay behind with our high school-aged kids, and if he was accepted, he would travel back and forth on weekends from wherever he'd be posted.

In our prayers, we expressed to God we didn't doubt His plan for us, we'd accept whatever decision came our way, and with His love and guidance, felt unequivocally assured all would be well. We determined if Randy's application was approved and the posting was no further than 250 km from home, he'd take the position, but if the offered posting was too far from his loved ones, he'd search for a new profession. While we were confident in God's ability to care for us, our heads were swimming with a myriad of emotions and all the possible outcomes of our dilemma. One Bible verse that's always struck a nerve in me is: *"So don't worry about tomorrow, for tomorrow will bring its own worries. Today's trouble is enough for today"* (Matthew 6:34).

In the past, Randy and I would have frantically worried and probably panicked about the pending result. Thankfully, we had spiritually matured and were deep into our refinement process as God's precious gems. It seemed like eons had passed since the harrowing, anxious days of the lawyer bill and owning two houses however, an optimistic calm hovered over our circumstances and we were mindful whatever the answer may be, God would be there with us, holding our hands.

My guy and I used this ordeal as an opportunity to show God our commitment and just how much we relied on Him and His mercy for us. Solomon wrote: *"Commit your actions to the Lord, and your plans will succeed"* (Proverbs 16:3). We prayed God would orchestrate a favourable contract for Randy and profusely thanked Him for all the blessings he'd already provided for us.

Our family unmistakably sensed God's love when Randy got the message that not only had he been received back into the full-time Canadian Armed Forces, but was being posted not too far away! We counted ourselves privileged as two other retired military members he had worked with were denied re-entry into their trade and had to look for alternate careers. And on top of that, we wholeheartedly felt our faithfulness was rewarded when this new appointment included a sizable bonus that made up for much of my lost wages. God is so good.

I know God heard our urgent plea and was proud of us because we went to Him with our problem rather than try to take it on ourselves. An uncertainty that could have easily been a source of turmoil and angst was peacefully and attentively handled through the everlasting love of our Father. But as with all solved problems, another one typically arises. At that point, I put a call out for some serious prayer knowing I was going to be caring for three teenagers by myself and was desperately hoping I wouldn't lose my sanity while doing it.

# WORTH EVERY PENNY

Chapter Nineteen

RANDY AND I WORKED TIRELESSLY ON STAYING WITHIN OUR means, not buying what we didn't need, balancing our credit card bill each month, not living to excess, and carefully outlining and saving for the future. Our diligence over the years has undeniably paid off and we are genuinely appreciating the fruits of our labour.

With God by our side, we never worry about money anymore knowing He will always provide for us. We live in true faith that His plan is perfect and get a delicious thrill out of sharing all He's given to us with the discouraged and defeated.

A very exorbitant purchase in our past included a trip to Cuba for our entire crew. This purchase however, came at a very different phase in our commitment to God as by then we were completely devoted to trusting Him with our finances and every other aspect of our lives. We had been tithing with joyous hearts and felt confident He would support our desire to take our children on a surprise, fun-filled vacation.

We'd been consistently serving others by sharing what we had and knew God was looking out for us in return by bestowing the funds needed to undertake this deluxe adventure. I'm certain God celebrates right along with us during exciting events and loves it when we dare to dream big. Our eldest son Luc was leaving home for the first time and jetting off to join the Air Force right after Christmas and his father and I wanted to have one last trip with him and his brother and sister before he left.

The heart of a mother is one of the most fascinating gifts to creation. From the moment of her child's conception to the minute she takes her last breath, a mother's heart is subconsciously engrossed with thoughts of her child and is constantly metamorphosing. First day of school, first time driving alone, heading off to college, getting married and having a baby of their own, are all milestones in which a mother's heart has no choice but to change into something different, but she doesn't know what and she doesn't know how. Harrowing, often uncontrollable emotions like worry and fear can accompany the transfiguration and it can be a raw and arduous process.

It's an odd feeling to have a part of your heart living outside your body. Wherever our children are, that is where our heart is also and when they leave home for the first time, jubilant with optimistic aspirations, a piece of your identity goes with them. And while every mother's greatest wish is that her child's life overflows with blessings and their road be straight, that's seldom the case. Broken relationships, job loss, illness, injury, and addiction riddle our kid's lives and it's emotionally painful to witness them suffer and to see their tears.

But there is hope. God has a perfect plan for your child too. It was difficult for me to comprehend at first because I thought there was nothing stronger than the bond between a mother and her child, but God also loves our children—even more than we do. Your child was created for a predestined purpose and as parents it should be our goal to help them walk in the right direction. I have learned to release a little of my maternal grip on my children and offer them up to God—trusting He can protect them in ways I never can and believing my support and constant motherly prayers will assist them in becoming all God has created them to be.

For the first time ever, I didn't buy the children any gifts for Christmas. Not one thing. I wrapped three empty boxes, one for each kid, and put them under the tree for appearance's sake. We called the children to the sofa for a short chat. The dreaded "family meetings" over the years usually consisted of reprimands and negative consequences for poor decisions, heated discussions about the cardinal rule of working together as a cohesive unit, animated debates about report cards and the importance of getting good grades, and serious matters such as moving, life decisions, and death. The kids never greeted these grievous gatherings with open arms and this instance wasn't any different.

As Randy and I sat our darling youngsters down in the living room on Christmas Eve, it was everything I could do not to burst into giggles as I took in the sombre looks on their faces. Our whole family had inherited a strong sense of humour, so in a very dismal tone my better half started the conversation by informing Luc, Jes, and Dev there wouldn't be any presents to open the next morning. The temperature in the room dropped as all six confused eyes looked under the tree at the fake gifts and then slowly turned to me. I could see all the wheels of cognition turning in their cute little heads. What about the gifts under the tree? What is Dad talking about? Why are we not getting presents?

I went to the tree, retrieved the three reindeer-papered boxes and gave one to each child. Perplexed by their light weight, they immediately tore into them and stared open-mouthed at their emptiness. I couldn't hold back for even one more second and gleefully announced the reason they weren't getting any presents was because we were going to Cuba...the next day! I still remember their shocked expressions as they processed the information. Instantly, the room erupted into euphoric chatter and jumps of joy. But because Randy and I had always been economically sensible, and while it definitely wasn't our objective to burst their bubble of enthusiasm, we explained to the children that the trip would come with a small price.

All three kids were working and each had quite a bit of cash in the bank and my spouse and I wanted to reiterate, once again, that *things* in life weren't free. Because we were travelling in high season, this trip was almost twice as much as it would have been later in the winter, and while we didn't exactly need their money, we figured they should chip in a tad and asked each child for $350 to help with the added expenses of the super fun excursions we'd take on our holiday.

No one even batted an eye. They all eagerly agreed and ran for their suitcases. Randy and I encountered a few raised eyebrows for even asking them to pitch in, but we stood by our intention and believed that a modest $350 contribution was worth its future weight in money management gold.

Our party of five ended up having a wonderful last vacation together, but as I watched my dear firstborn laugh and frolic around the pool with his siblings, a heavy sense of melancholy plagued my heart realizing he was flying the coop right after we got home. Nevertheless, I felt comforted in knowing Luc had been raised with a strongly anchored foundation based on love and Christian morals and would carry his knowledge about budgeting, debt, and investments with him into the vast, wide world of "adulting."

# WHAT'S THE PLAN?

Chapter Twenty

THE OLD ADAGE "I WISH I'D HAVE KNOWN THEN WHAT I KNOW now" comes to mind when I recall my employment opportunities over the years. God always has our best interest at heart but blessings can sometimes come disguised as difficulties. Many events happen in life that we can't understand; ordinary occurrences like not getting the apology we deserve, or monumental instances such as the miscarriage of our first baby. While these burdens are often impossible to comprehend, through God's eyes we learn to realize, and put into context, they're all part of a bigger and better plan for us. Humankind is not meant to know everything about their lives. The prophet Jeremiah wrote, *"'For I know the plans I have for you,' says the Lord. 'They are plans for good and not for disaster, to give you a future and a hope'"* (Jeremiah 29:11).

We are meant to submit everything to God and to rely on Him for the outcome. Once I applied for a job I would have been remarkably suited for. I was overly competent in the field and was more than educationally qualified. After submitting my request to God I awaited the company's reply. I thought, without a doubt, the position was going to be mine and had my entire wardrobe and lunchbox meals arranged accordingly. Not only didn't I get the job, they didn't even give me an interview. I was crushed.

What I didn't see back then, but now understand, was God said "no." For some reason I might never know, the position wasn't right for me and God knew it. He loved me so much He denied my request in order to either protect me from harm or bring me a much better offer. God's way is perfect. It always has been and always will be.

It became obvious to me God truly did want to give me my heart's desire when I decided to join the Canadian Forces alongside my husband. I had desperately yearned to be an "army girl" ever since I saw Goldie Hawn portray *Private Benjamin* at age 10 and it had always been my life-long dream to be a soldier. I looked into enlisting when I was 17 but wasn't bold enough to do it. Then Randy and I got married, I had our babies and motherhood happened.

It's uncanny how movie stars can have so much in-fluence on our lives. After watching Demi Moore play a butt-kicking Navy Special Warfare trainee in *G.I. Jane*, my vision was refueled and I visited the recruiting centre again when I was 30. I had just completed the full application process when I chickened out and withdrew my name, again. Apparently the passion inside me didn't die because I prayed and prayed and cried and begged God to let me fulfill my never-ending drive to nobly wear a uniform every day for my country. Finally, probably because He was getting tired of me bugging Him, God said "Yes!"

When we start to see God as our Father, a father that loves us unconditionally as opposed to just our big boss in the sky, we start to appreciate the inconceivable goodness of His will and design for us. And while we can never entirely see His big picture and what the ultimate intention for our life is, God created His plan for us before we were born and that's why His answer is oftentimes "no." But at age 35, I raced off to join the military leaving Luc, Jesse, and Devin for more than a weekend for the very first time since they were born. Basic training was a lengthy and gruelling endeavour but I actively kept engaged with God, through sweat, pulled muscles, and tears, and asked Him to stand by my side and make me strong and courageous.

He heard my all-or-nothing pleas and did just that. I graduated from basic training with the Top Athlete Award, beating out 44 other contenders including many very young and physically fit men and women. While a top athlete is often rewarded for their peak athletic ability, I was informed I was nominated above all other candidates because of my unwavering determination, my ability to encourage others, and my refusal to give up. As excruciating as it was, and as much as I missed my family, I enjoyed completing my goal and was so happy that God never left my side.

However, it wasn't long before I discovered the Canadian Forces weren't a good fit for me and thought it so ironic that something I'd prayed so persistently for over the years didn't wind up being what was best for me after all. I didn't end up getting the career selection I'd originally signed up for and Randy and I were unexpectedly posted to a base far from where we presumed we were going. And to add even more fuel to the fire, this was the exact moment we were carrying that double-mortgage too. Life just kept tossing us one curve ball after another.

I couldn't see why, after all of the preparation and praying I'd done, everything was turning out to be the exact opposite of what I'd envisioned. After some intense discussion and prayer, I ended up releasing from the military and Randy chose to retire, taking on the full-time reservist contract. But I do not regret, even for one minute, my stint as a soldier. I'm still so elated, even to this day, I completed such a movie-worthy and valiant feat and am so proud of my daring accomplishment.

As I was surprised by the reality my life-long fantasy didn't turn out to be part of God's plan for me, I had to ask Him why. "Why did You let me join the military when You knew it wasn't right for me? Why did You allow me to go through all that hard work and hardship just to find out it wasn't the career that I'd hoped it would be?" My whole community had been cheering me on and there was even a newspaper article about me entitled "My Mom Wears Army Boots." I was ashamed. Embarrassment followed me around like a gloomy cloud; I felt like I had let everyone down and that people thought I was a quitter.

Disappointment haunted my mind. While I was ecstatic to be home again and relieved not to be moving across the country, my emotions betrayed me and confusion addled my thoughts so heavily I asked my pastor for his insight. His response astounded me. I fully believe the Spirit of God put the words directly in my pastor's mouth when he said in some ways he considers God to be just like any other father—except He's God, of course. He loved me so much, wanted to wrap His arms around me, and grant me my childhood aspiration. While He knew the profession wasn't right for me, I didn't know it, and just kept pestering and praying for years and years and years for Him to allow my request.

God knew joining the military wouldn't hurt me in any way. It would force me into fearless confidence I'd never possessed before, produce opportunities for me to tell others about God's love, increase my faith to previously unreached heights, and allow me a glimpse into the occupation my husband had so proudly dedicated his life to. So He patted me on my cute little head and lovingly sent me on my way so I'd experience for myself just exactly what it was He was saying "no" to. Once I heard this analogy from my pastor, I fell deeper in love with God on the spot. The Apostle John reminds us, *"For this is how God loved the world: He gave his one and only Son, so that everyone who believes in him will not perish but have eternal life"* (John 3:16).

That's a pretty big love and there are no words to express how intensely loved I felt knowing God approved my greatest wish even though He knew it wasn't His ultimate direction for me and yet, still graced me with His unconditional protection. That's what He did for me and that is what He'll do for everyone who turns to Him, puts their dependence in Him, and lives each day according to His life-giving Word.

# MULTIPLY
# AND SAVE

Chapter Twenty-One

Once upon a time, I unrealistically tried to tally up a dollar amount of all I'd saved over the years by being cautious with our purchases. It was impossible to calculate a definitive number but I presumed it was somewhere between four and five thousand dollars a year when I took into account the steadfast fervour and devotion I'd committed to making my undertaking a success.

But as much as the Leighton team was invested in our mission of frugality and were reaping the benefits by going on many day trips and vacations, I gave up on my effort to come up with a grand total. Because we'd been living modestly for so many years, sensibility and sound judgement with our spending had become second nature to us; it was a significant aspect of our shared philosophy and certainly didn't feel like a chore. We saved what we could whenever the window presented itself, and always looked for other ways to cut all unnecessary costs.

As a military member, my serviceman has gotten a haircut every two weeks for 32 years. Early on in his career, Randy regularly visited the barber for bi-monthly trims. The cost of haircuts quickly added up and before long he wisely obtained his own set of hair clippers. For the past three decades, my hubby has cut his own hair and whenever possible had his beautiful assistant—that would be me—touch up any areas he'd missed.

> cost of a haircut
> × every two weeks
> × 29 years
> = money saved

While hanging all those cutie-pie cloth diapers on the clothes line summer after summer, I purchased an indoor drying rack and began to hang our entire family's clothes on it throughout the fall and winter too. I dried everything in the dryer for ten minutes to get the wrinkles out and then either hung it outside or on the rack. And for the last ten years, I've been making my own homemade laundry detergent and fabric softener too. I originally started because I had become scent sensitive and it was suggested I make the transition from commercial products to a more natural or organic substitute, but what began as a way to protect the health of myself and my loved ones promptly became evident as a money saving tactic too.

$$\begin{aligned} &\text{cost of using the dryer} \\ \times\ &\text{price of commercial laundry aids} \\ \times\ &\text{10-25 years} \\ =\ &\text{money saved} \end{aligned}$$

As I've cooked from scratch for most of my married life, avoided overvalued prepackaged foods as much as I could, and always scoured the "reduced" racks for bargains, I've saved thousands on our grocery bills. I baked muffins and handcrafted trail mix for snacks as opposed to buying boxed bars; I've always made my own chicken broth to have an inexpensive meal idea at my fingertips; and I scheduled delicious, budget-conscious meals four or five times a week to keep our food costs low.

> cost of packaged foods
> × weekly grocery shopping
> × 29 years
> = money saved

Another way we multiplied our funds over the years was by taking every chance to pay off our houses as fast as we could. Practically every cent I ever made was immediately deposited on our mortgage, and with every additional amount that came our way, either from income tax refunds or financial blessings from God, rather than running out and buying meaningless and unplanned things, we took advantage of the occasion by decreasing our mortgage debt even further.

> my income and blessing money
> × avoided mortgage interest
> × 20 years
> = money saved

Thankfully, Randy has a bit of automotive knowledge and has put it to very good use over the years. As the cost of getting work done by mechanics can be quite expensive, rather than take our vehicles to a garage, my guy saved us a bundle by changing the oil in our vehicles himself and using our driveway to transfer the summer and winter tires each season. He also made sure to keep our vehicles continually well-maintained in order to get as many years out of them as we possibly could.

tire transfers
× oil changes and maintenance
× 30 years
= money saved

While I could probably list a dozen more ways we've saved our cash, I'll just share one more. On every vacation we've ever taken that wasn't all-inclusive, we always booked a hotel room with a kitchen to cook our own food and avoid restaurant costs. We've taken oatmeal and Baby-Bel cheese to Bali, brought a frying pan to Las Vegas, packed our suitcase with uncooked rice and protein powder for Arizona, and bought a Styrofoam cooler in Hawaii to keep our yogurt and veggies cold. We limited and slated our restaurant days according to our outings and have saved thousands upon thousands of dollars in the process.

convenient travel foods

× foreign restaurant costs

× always

= money saved

Our family has been saving money for so long it's instinctive to us and we never think twice about our conservation practices. We consider them to be an everyday part of our life and we're grateful to God for always giving us the inclination to make wise choices. Remember, *"For the Lord grants wisdom! From his mouth come knowledge and understanding"* (Proverbs 2:6).

And we know the Bible is the Word of God, so the more we read it, the better our lives get. Our only regret is we didn't study it sooner!

# PAYING FOR PREMIUM

Chapter Twenty-Two

As a newlywed and young mother, it had always been my ambition to have enough funds to grocery shop at a premium store in the city. You know what store I mean. The one with the wide, clean aisles. The store with the most gorgeous fruits and veggies you've ever seen. The one that costs significantly more but is indisputably worth it because of its serene atmosphere and many available cashiers.

Our cupboards had been stocked by lower-end stores for so many years and what I wanted, above all else, was for that high-class supermarket to be my primary grocery store. I burned with a desire to walk in like I owned the place and put whatever suited my fancy in the cart, with no regard to the cost. Unfortunately, this superior store came with sky-high prices and was always too expensive for our budget-friendly clan. That changed when we were finished carrying that double-mortgage and I was earning a modest but respectable salary in the Canadian Forces. I was determined I was switching grocery stores.

For the first time in our married lives, Randy and I had some real money; enough to go into the rich-people store and grab anything we pleased. In order to thoroughly take in every benefit "Grocery Store Heaven" had to offer, I waited until my day off and went armed with an arsenal of reusable shopping bags and a very full list. It was just as I'd anticipated it would be when I walked through the front doors: the produce section was aglow with a divine, heavenly aura, the gleaming aisles were paved with brilliant gold, and the angels were singing, ever so sweetly, on the overhead store radio. Oh my.

My vision of becoming one of those unhurried shoppers who just saunter lazily around the store was blissfully coming true. After literally stopping to smell God's beautiful roses, I checked my list, spotted my first target, and headed on over.

Bananas were the number one fruit staple in our home and as I grabbed my second bunch, I peeked at the tag, which read $.89/lb. I was a little taken aback and thought they must be the organic variety as my usual discount store sold bananas for only $.47/lb. They turned out to be just regular, everyday bananas and $.89/lb was the price. Right away, my heart and head entered into a mini-debate but my heart won out because I was finally in my dream store and overjoyed to be there.

Next on my list were apples. We each took an apple in our lunch almost every day and I needed two large bags to last us the week. As I glanced around the produce section to find the brand we liked, I was shocked by what they were charging! As other happy-go-lucky customers casually shopped around me, freely filling their carts with astronomically-priced fruits and cream of the crop vegetables, I just stood there in the middle of the aisle and came to a bubble-bursting conclusion. Even our favourite apples cost nearly twice as much as they did at my no-extra-frills grocery store!

I looked down at my oversized list and quickly tallied up the added amount I'd be required to shell out just to get whatever I wanted. Life is sometimes like that. We want what we want, when we want it, and exactly how we want it. We completely disregard all common sense and take matters into our own hands with no thought of God and His previous-laid plans for us. We become proud and selfish and assume we're smarter than God in what is right and best for us.

Unfortunately, there's a grim price to pay for throwing everything you hunger for into your cart. We can't have it both ways where we haphazardly toss all our whims and wishes into our cart and then expect God to pay for it. God calls us to live in an atmosphere of expectancy where He will fulfill the desires of our hearts if only we will abide in harmonious agreement with His perfectly designed intent for us. For Mark reminds us: *"And you must love the Lord your God with all your heart, all your soul, all your mind, and all your strength"* (Mark 12:30).

When we put God first, everything else falls into place. Things may not always turn out as we'd envisioned them but when we really know Him, His strengths, what He's done in the past, and what the Bible tells us about eternity, we don't worry about the future because His unmistakable love for us never ceases or fails.

As I blankly stood there in front of the array of elite apples, I suddenly decided I was not willing to pay the price of shopping at that heavenly store. I put my bananas back on the shelf, grabbed the carrots I knew were on sale, and high-tailed it out of there. As I walked through the doors of my regular discount store, I was cheered by its familiarity and relieved I wouldn't be wasting any money that day on frivolous purchases. I did grab a nice bouquet of fragrant yellow roses however (that were exactly half the amount of those at the premium store), as a high-five to God for always being there for our family.

I know many double-income families make enough to buy high-end clothes, have two ritzy cars, habitually dine out, and own all the latest gadgets, but that's never been our experience. When Randy and I first got married, I had to get a job right away in order for us to afford our rent, car loan, and insurance. We were struggling from paycheque to paycheque and had no savings. We were only able to start putting a little away into an RRSP after I'd been working for a couple of years and my army man got his first large raise.

As the babies came and we became single-income again, it was mandatory for us to keep our costs low and mindfully note each and every detail of our budget. It was a rare occasion when my sweetheart and I ever entertained the notion of having more. We were always content with what we had and didn't feel we were missing out on anything, even when I had to minimize our grocery list to help us survive until payday.

Our family has come a long way in our finances. While we aren't likely to be classified as filthy rich, our list of needs has always been relatively simple and that's allowed us the ability to make a few large purchases and take memorable vacations.

Needs and wants are two very different things though and I acquired yet another valuable lesson some years back when I attempted to buy our teenage daughter some boots for Christmas. These spiffy boots were becoming more popular and Devin had expressed an interest in owning a pair. But when we heard the price of these posh boots, we immediately squashed the idea of buying them as it would have been more than twice the amount we'd typically spend on one gift.

As the holidays drew closer and I still didn't have a special gift for Dev, we gave the thought of the high-class boots some more consideration and decided we would get them for her but that they'd be part of her birthday gift too. The initial cash output would be morally difficult, but at least I'd have her birthday taken care of and Devin would get the object of her affection.

Randy and I went to the shoe store with the full intention of coming out with a new pair of designer boots to surprise our darling daughter. However, when we got to the display and looked again at the ludicrous sticker amount, we absolutely, positively, couldn't bring ourselves to buy them. It wasn't that we couldn't afford the boots; we could. Mentally, and in the pits of our stomachs, we refused to misuse that much of our hard-earned riches on a fashion article just so our daughter could sport smokin' hot boots and keep up with the Kardashians—the more modern version of the Joneses. We ended up getting Devin some great, more practical, gifts for Christmas and her birthday and she was none the wiser.

About a month after her birthday, Devin brought up the topic of the exclusive boots she had craved so much. She told us she'd originally wanted them when they first became popular but was glad she didn't get them because by then, every girl she knew had a pair. My husband and I locked eyes, smiled with relief, and proceeded to tell Dev about our adventure to the shoe store and how quickly we dismissed the thought of indulging in such a pointless purchase.

We were able to share with her the wisdom we'd gained that day: even if you can afford something, it doesn't mean you should be coerced into buying it. Her dad and I had recognized the temptation of commercialism and were honoured to pass our rationality down to our daughter.

# DECISIONS, DECISIONS...

Chapter Twenty-Three

THERE HAVE BEEN HUNDREDS OF TIMES WHEN OUR FAMILY could have spent more money but chose not to. The flip side is there have also been many times we could have chosen to spend less but didn't. What you do with your wages should be a decision-making process and not just a mindless pursuit to fulfil your every wish.

When faced with an upcoming purchase, Randy and I typically made sure the item was a need and not just a want, weighed the pros and cons, read reviews, and based our verdict on many factors. Impulse buying results in consumers getting stuff they really don't have cause for and a big bill they didn't allot for, and we're relieved we can claim victory over the draw of it.

I can't even remember the last time we have bought something without thinking about it first. As I'm now doing more online shopping than ever before—and unde- niably appreciate the technology—it's so easy to see how buyers can get themselves into serious debt. Your credit card number has already been inputted into the website and within two clicks, one to "add to cart" and one to "checkout," you've added another charge to your monthly credit card statement!

This may or may not have been a purchase that was truly essential but the soul-sucking question is could you really afford it? I'm grateful I haven't become obsessed with the online, mail order mania and am still conscientious, even as an empty-nester, of our continued motivation to safeguard our wallets.

Randy and I still take a lunch in the car and rarely buy snacks while out and about, but are still in the process of learning that in order to make the best possible choic- es and to do what's best for our bank account, every now and again we need to spend more than we'd anticipated. For the past thirty years, my hubby has always been very fortunate when buying our used vehicles by praying first, then shopping around, checking reviews, and negotiating accordingly. We were reflecting the other day that in all of the years of vehicle buying, we have never been saddled with a lemon. Thank you God!

Throughout our marriage, we've only ever owned one new vehicle and to be truthful, it was an enlightening experience for us. When I was doing full-time home child-care and regularly transporting five children, while in the process of searching for a van to replace our aging one, we decided a new one would best suit our requirements. I was making a pretty good wage at that point and this new van had many bells and whistles, seated eight passengers, was ideal for daycare, had a tonne of room for hockey bags, and had a bigger engine with an extended towing package to pull our camper. It was the first new vehicle we ever had and we liked owning something modern and fresh.

What we didn't like, however, was the expense. It was a pretty indulgent van and our monthly payments were spread out over five years. It hurt to see that huge sum withdrawn every month and we definitely felt it. While we loved our van, all the adventures it took our tribe on and the wonderful memories it created for us, Randy and I determined that "new" came with a price, a hefty added cost, and we probably wouldn't make that choice again.

After the van, we resumed scouring the Internet for used cars for several years until Randy moved away to his employment posting and I stayed home with the children. While in the market for another vehicle, we prayerfully elected to lease a car for the first time. As my health wasn't great and I was still raising teens, Randy was uneasy about me having the additional responsibility of frequently taking an older car to a garage for repairs while he was away but with a leased car, my soldier's concerns were nonexistent as any necessary repairs were cared for by the dealership.

The decision to lease worked well for us and we know God agreed because we specifically asked Him about it before making our selection. When people put God first above all else, lives change dramatically. Life falls right into place when God is invited to have His hand in it and to be our guiding light.

Mankind often displays mysterious priorities. A priority is defined as something that's regarded as more important and takes precedence over something else. I've always been dumbfounded by families who say they can't afford something when what they really mean is they refuse to cut their blow-it-all habits to pay for it. People have money for what they want to have money for and personal sacrifice and willpower must be part of an adult's conduct if they ever strive to achieve true monetary gain.

Our family used the library instead of purchasing books, took a lunch instead of eating out, and saved for items other than lottery tickets (if you invest just $50 per month as opposed to buying tickets, you could accrue about $50,000 in 30 years). And because we've been including God in our financial plans, we now have a little extra for a few of the finer things in life. It's easy to find peace in your purchases when you've gone to God first. To be honest, neither Randy nor I feel we've sacrificed much over the past 29 years; we just lived within our means and were careful with the money God provided to us.

An indispensable priority for our entourage, which may have seemed unwarranted to some, was our decision to hire a housekeeper to help with our chores. Shortly after I started into full-time home childcare, I became very run-down and extremely worn out. Back then, my honey was working very lengthy shifts, was often away for weeks on end, and Luc, Jes, and Dev were all heavily involved with school events and hockey. I was working more than 50 hours a week and was physically and mentally exhausted. Our evenings were bursting at the seams with family bonding time and a host of extracurricular activities, and our jam-packed weekends included hockey, endless birthday parties, and church. Not only was I cleaning up after my own herd but constantly tidying after five toddlers too. Our own children had their fair share of chores of course, but something had to give.

We looked into the cost of hiring a cleaner and how much freedom I'd acquire by doing so. Our intention was to try it for a few months before committing to any type of contract but we immediately discovered it was one of the most brilliant ideas we'd ever had! While we did have to free up some of our hard-earned cash, we were richly rewarded with the precious extra seconds we now had to hang out with our kids and relax for five minutes.

It was vital that one of us was always home for our children (which having the home daycare permitted me to do) and everything ran much more efficiently when the housekeeper walked through our door. Our priority was our family, not our money, and God blessed us enough to be able to afford some much-needed and well-deserved relief.

# SPEND TO SAVE

Chapter Twenty-Four

ON OUR BLISSFUL BUT WILD PARENTHOOD ADVENTURE, Randy and I tried to pass on a wealth of financial intelligence to our children whenever the opportunity presented itself. When the kids started school, I wasn't forced to participate in the back-to-school shopping frenzy as I super-sleuthed second-hand clothes throughout the year and most Christmases and birthdays overflowed with new clothing. But as the years passed and the kids discovered shopping, we would scout for deals at the outlet stores and take full advantage of the off-season sales.

Randy and I always gave Luc, Jes, and Dev a couple of bucks to purchase one new affordable outfit for the first of September, although we knew many families who dropped large wads of cash every fall for their kids to look cool and fit in. In my experience, boys aren't really aware of clothing trends until middle school age, but girls, I guess because of other little girls, often develop their sense of self in their primary years and can quickly become slaves to fashion.

Glamour magazines used to be the front-running cause of poor self-image and our confidence was often trampled by the unattainable beauty of the supermodels. But over the past dozen years or so, social media has usurped their authority and has no problem making women of all ages feel inferior to what they see online. We perceive our motherhood leaves much to be desired, our home looks nothing like what we see on HGTV, and our physical appearance—regardless of our reflection in a full-length mirror—is not good enough.

It grieves me that society can be so cruel. Racism, discrimination, and hardheartedness are rampant in this world and it may sound naïve but if everyone would just follow the instruction of Jesus to love one another, this broken planet could receive the healing it so desperately needs. I always tried to set a positive example and worked tirelessly on teaching our children to look beyond what they could see—skin colour, clothes, and first impressions—and get to know someone personally; a value I know they still hold today.

Since the day Devin was born, I made every attempt to impress upon her that true beauty is a product of the heart, to be confident in who she is, and the importance of not being perceived as a show off. You are to *"...clothe yourselves instead with the beauty that comes from within, the unfading beauty of a gentle and quiet spirit, which is so precious to God"* (1 Peter 3:4).

Now, I'm pretty sure no one would ever accuse Devin or I of being overly quiet, but I hope I've successfully passed on the idea that others shouldn't dictate what we wear. I always told Devin if something appeals to her, she should wear it with confidence and not be bothered by the opinions of others, and it's alright to want to look nice, but to be sure her clothes are not too revealing and of good quality. Good quality? Yes, good quality. I figured out, the hard way, that inexpensive rarely means better and money is easily wasted by buying cheaply manufactured items.

On an exciting, ladies-only weekend getaway, I got caught up in the hustle and bustle and Christmas shopping hype and did something completely out of character. I treated myself to a purse. A very pretty purse. A $125 purse. Without any previous research or forethought! Oh my. I'd never had a purse of such sophistication before and bought it entirely on a whim. It was a beautiful shoulder bag and I loved carrying it around on the rest of my girl's trip.

However, upon returning home, the guilt set in and I couldn't believe I'd spent that much on such an impractical thing. I presumed Randy would question my indulgence but he didn't. He just laughed a bit, undoubtedly because I'd always been so frugal, and wished me a Merry Christmas. At first, I was embarrassed to be carrying around such a flashy leather bag but then realized I was in the midst of acquiring another treasured tidbit of wisdom.

I'd always bought cheap purses. Not only were they inexpensive but most were poorly made from low quality materials. While I don't think I'm the type of person that needs to make a fashion statement with name brand accessories, this new addition was magnificent. In the past, I'd buy a handbag from a discount store only to have it fray and fall apart within six months. I'd then drag that tattered relic around for a couple more months before going on the hunt for another one.

A little while after buying my designer Christmas handbag, I became sorely aware I'd been inadvertently wasting my money on bargain-basement purses. Even after repeatedly banging it off the van door and tossing it around the hockey bleachers for almost a year, the quality of my carry-everything-that-will-fit tote stood up to the rigours of life as a busy working mom and still looked as new as the day I got it. In fact, I was so impressed with the workmanship of the brand, I only wrote one thing on my wish list the following Christmas, and Randy bought me another high-quality cross-body bag in a different colour.

A few months after getting my swanky new purse I was able to pass on my revolutionary knowledge of low-quality goods to my daughter. Every spring, my husband would take our sons on a weekend fishing trip and my girl and I would travel to the city for some no-boys-allowed reconnection.

Devin was in the market for a new pair of black dress pants and after shopping around we narrowed the search down to two options: one pair at a mass-market store (poor quality) for $20 and one pair from a smaller fashion store (good quality) for $40. Dev was nearing the end of her growing stage and was in search of a pair of pants that would last long-term and as she had already used the cash I'd given her as a treat, she was purchasing them with her own money.

Because Devin was paying out of her own pocket, she was definitely leaning toward the cheaper pants. From first-hand expertise and the appearance of the pants, I knew they probably wouldn't even make it out of the washing machine before they'd be ruined. I took advantage of the teaching moment and gently explained why she should buy the better pants. She was apprehensive, as she was always mindful with her bank account, but at least trusted me enough to heed my advice. In the end, she was at ease with her purchase and thankfully grasped the invaluable lesson that now and again you need to spend money to save money.

My new purse adventure was just another example of how I determined that cheaper isn't better. Also, I fully maintain God wants His children to enjoy their lives. I'd never placed any stock in letting material things control my contentment but I truly liked and appreciated my new handbag. I had dedicated so many years to meticulously saving and conserving, tithing, blessing others, and carefully economizing every single thing, I think God was happy that I was happy. Wise King Solomon once wrote: *"And people should eat and drink and enjoy the fruits of their labor, for these are gifts from God"* (Ecclesiastes 3:13).

It's important to note happiness is only a temporary emotion based on your external circumstances while true joy is a deep feeling of gratitude and the attitude of your heart. Taking the initiative to thrive is up to us and we should all aspire to live with an enthusiastic sense of joy.

Many people experience unimaginably dire situations and even though darkness lingers all around them, the unshakable joy in their spirit helps to light their way. If our eyes are open to it, we can delight in the world's beauty, see the absolute best in everyone and everything, and blissfully and unreservedly embrace, and be thankful for, the priceless gifts God grants to us each and every day.

# FAITH
# WITHOUT FEAR

Chapter Twenty-Five

ONE OF THE GREATEST CONFIRMATIONS OF OUR FAITH IN GOD'S love for us occurred during our last real estate transaction. Buying and selling homes is stressful but with God in the contract, it can be smooth sailing and worry-free.

When Randy first retired from the Canadian Forces in 2008, we helped a contractor build a large, beautiful house for us in our childhood town. As Randy and I fully expected it to be our retirement home and that we'd reside there for at least thirty more years, the materials and fixtures we installed were somewhat more expensive than what we'd have used if we'd known we would move again. Most people have preconceived notions of what their lives will be like. Ha! I love the old Yiddish proverb that says, "Man plans, God laughs!"

After God approved my spouse's desire to re-enlist in the Canadian Forces, we mutually decided we were comfortable with him attempting to complete another ten years as a member. Although our plans were to live in our new abode forever, God's plan was entirely different and it included surrendering the project we had worked so very, very hard on. Because the house was a bit more affluent than most other residences in our neighbourhood, Randy and I knew we were going to need a special buyer with a large budget to become its new owner.

While we were always satisfied with the attractive home we had created through blood, twelve-hour workdays, and stressed-out tears, we felt a bit troubled when some referred to it as fancy. We were well aware our property delivered amazing curb appeal but as Randy and I had already adopted a spirit of humility, it unnerved us to know we may have been considered show-offs over its grandeur appearance. Jeremiah proclaimed to Israel: *"This is what the Lord says: 'Don't let the wise boast in their wisdom, or the powerful boast in their power, or the rich boast in their riches'"* (Jeremiah 9:23).

Even though we knew we weren't boastful people, we didn't like to be perceived as such and were seriously mulling over the idea that our next dwelling, wherever it may be, would represent more of the humble and modest example we were interested in portraying.

Six months before putting our house up for sale, our family began praying for God to have His hand in the upcoming agreement. We prayed God would prepare the right buyer for us and that the sale would go off without a hitch. Randy and I had complete confidence in God, knowing and believing everything would work out exactly according to His plan and not ours. We prayed for our buyer every day throughout that fall and winter.

When the time to sell rolled around, we chose an acquaintance of ours, also a Christian, to become our real estate agent. According to market assessment our house was worth $80,000 less than what we had put into it! Oh my. While we knew God had promised to take care of us, our worldly hearts pounded in our chests. We had already suffered numerous losses in real estate deals and admittedly didn't want to start from scratch again, cancelling out all the diligent saving and recovering we'd done over the years. Then we recognized we were letting a fear into our lives that didn't belong there. While we could have easily entered a state of unsettled worry and alarm, we chose to trust God.

Our agent suggested a starting figure and we added $10,000 more for good measure. At that point, the asking price was already $50,000 less than our original output and we were vigilantly trying to remember that whatever the outcome, God really did have everything under control. Randy and I didn't have our heads in the clouds and knew, with certainty, our home was going to be a difficult sell. We just kept remembering when Jesus said: *"I tell you, you can pray for anything, and if you believe that you've received it, it will be yours"* (Mark 11:24).

Our faith didn't waiver in the least. We were confident God was the commander-in-chief of this endeavour and had a wonderful resolution for us. We didn't even allow ourselves to be discouraged by the fact there was only one other house in our local area in the same price range as ours and it had been on the market for more than two years. We just kept on praying, believing, trusting, and obeying.

When our property didn't even have one interested party in the first couple months, Randy and I dropped the asking price $10,000 to where our agent originally stated it would be best. Within the next month, we had an offer on our home. Sadly, it was a low proposal that caused a lot of unwelcome tension but we were blessed to have a real estate agent who also stood firm on his belief that God would provide for both our goals and his, and deliver the assurance we needed to close the deal.

As this low offer was the only one we'd seen, Randy and I determined it was in our best interest to not totally dissuade the buyer. Our counter offer was significantly higher than the buyer's pitch but unfortunately, he wasn't willing to budge very far from his initial amount. The ironic detail that threw us into an even bigger quandary was the closing date for the impending sale was perfect for us and the proposed offer was not reliant on the buyer selling his place first. All we had to do was agree on a price and the deal would be done.

Randy and I took our monumental decision before the throne of our Saviour. If we accepted the buyer's offer, we'd be agreeing to an amount that was $75,000 less than what we'd spent on the house. We couldn't forget that because we'd built a live-in-forever retirement home, we weren't going to sell for any amount even close to our initial output, but we were at least hoping boxed macaroni and cheese wouldn't become our number one food staple for the rest of our lives. But once again, we lifted our hands to our Heavenly Father and put our entire hope in Him. Our Holy Bible states:

> *Don't worry about anything; instead, pray about every-thing. Tell God what you need, and thank him for all he has done. Then you will experience God's peace, which exceeds anything we can understand. His peace will guard your hearts and minds as you live in Christ Jesus.*
> —Philippians 4:6-7

Randy and I had finally come to the realization, after years and years of thinking about money, that our bank account didn't belong to us. It was God's money He provided to us through job offers, unexpected windfalls, large tax refunds, and His never-ending love for us. We knew if we approved the offer, we would stand united with the Apostle Paul in his belief that God would supply all our needs.

With irrefutable peace, we accepted the buyer's final offer and our home sold in just over three months. Sure, we could have resorted to the nail-biting pressure of waiting the matter out for a higher offer, but we refused to go down that broken road again as it hadn't produced the best results for us in the past. I got to share with a few people about how God had orchestrated a buyer for us and even got to put a glory-filled shout out to Him on Facebook, thanking Him for taking care of us. I can't even fathom how different the outcome might have been if we hadn't included God in that transaction. Even though we lost money, we honestly, without reservation, felt richer than we'd ever been before.

# OUR BEST INVESTMENT

Chapter Twenty-Six

WE ONLY GET ONE PHYSICAL BODY AND WE ONLY GET ONE LIFE. It's our responsibility to take care of the body God gave us and the best investment we can ever make is in our health. Personal health has always been a priority for our family. It helped we couldn't afford to eat out and buy snacks at the arena, and the ready-to-eat and packaged meals never fit into our budget. I always outlined our menus and prepared healthy meals with the resources I had—but naturally still took occasional advantage of a frozen pizza on crazy hockey nights.

There's no refuting junk food consumption is detrimental to our health and today's meals aren't the same as the ones our grandparents ate. Terms like "nitrates," "butylated hydroxyanisole," and "propylene glycol" grace our nutrition labels and our genetically-modified food is laden with parabens, pesticides, artificial sweeteners, and chemically-created colouring. Our human bodies weren't designed to recognize these foreign substances and in turn, react accordingly. Poor diets lead to a terrible array of ailments and are linked to higher rates of obesity, depression, diabetes, and heart disease. We all know we feel bloated and sluggish after eating too much junk, so why on earth do we do that to our bodies?

When our gang did indulge, pop, chips, and chocolatey-goodness were saved for weekends and outings and we counteracted their effects with a unified commitment to physical fitness. With the kids in hockey, soccer, baseball, and track, that took care of both their sport and social involvement. As a service member, Randy has participated in physical training almost every morning of his 32-year career, and evenings and Saturdays satisfied his passion for hockey and golf. And as for me, I've always walked, biked, ran, went to Zumba, used the Wii for bustin' a move on Just Dance, or did an old-fashioned video tape at home. Plus, we often hiked together on Sundays after church where the kids would get a kick out of sharing their zany summer camp songs with us at the top of their lungs!

Another fundamental part of healthy living is our social life. Even though we made sure the kids always had the opportunity to be part of a circle or team through sports, youth group, clubs, and cousins, Randy and I never really put much stock into expanding our friend zone. Then we became empty-nesters.

When the kids left, they took their social agendas with them and we found ourselves in new territory with our silent rooms and blank calendar. It was strange. Chatting with other adults at the hockey rink was our connection to humanity and without them it seemed boring and bleak. We were so accustomed to the wild and mighty hurricane of parenthood that the aftermath felt eerily calm and still. My soldier was away for over half our marriage and not only had we moved to a new town and didn't know anybody, we barely knew each other either.

While it was wonderful to finally be spending time together after so many energy-zapping years of raising kids, it was also lonely for us as we hadn't found a church and didn't know where to meet people. The bar scene didn't appeal to us and we no longer fit into the parents-with-kids demographic. After trying out a handful of churches, we settled on a Bible-based one that offered lots of activities.

Randy and I met some great folks at our respective men's and ladies' groups and became immersed in our new church community within the first month. Social circles are vital for a healthy lifestyle. Some of the oldest cultures on the planet continue to thrive because they still eat together, pray together, and laugh together.

What we focus our attention on often determines our outlook on life. Pessimism adversely affects our well-being and it's imperative to have a positive, glass-half-full attitude. The alternative only hurts our heart and inhibits our growth. While we are not responsible for the actions of others, we are accountable for our own. Although it's always important to be kind, we don't need to dwell on the negativity and hurtful words we receive from others. There will always be someone that doesn't like you, choose not to be a part of your life, and oppose you because of your beliefs. And that's alright. We are so precious to God and He always wants us to focus on the truth of His love. Paul says: *"Fix your thoughts on what is true, and honorable, and right, and pure, and lovely, and admirable. Think about things that are excellent and worthy of praise"* (Philippians 4:8).

There's no denying we live in a shamefully cynical world. Society is overburdened with grumpy drivers, hot-headed sports fans, blatant selfishness, and social media bullies. Everyone thinks they are "right," resulting in argumentative natures and bad attitudes. They are blind to the wonderment of life and have no clue how to practice gratitude. Take every chance to embrace positivity as much as you can by looking on the bright side. Every situation has a blessing from God, and the more we trust Him, the easier it is to see it.

Ask any Christian who's been through a traumatic circumstance and they'll tell you, without reservation, their faith in God sustained them. Faith, what is it? *"Faith shows the reality of what we hope for; it is the evidence of things we cannot see"* (Hebrews 11:1).

Another way to describe faith is believing all God's promises will come true. It is an essential part of a healthy life and when trying to adopt a better way of living, or even just make a few changes, God can make transformations beyond anything you could dream. But first, you need to have faith. Share a cup of tea with someone of great faith and just see for yourself how contagious it is. It's hard to be depressed when you're around a person who has a strong devotion to God. While many try, willpower is not enough to make the integral changes necessary for the best possible results. Only God can accomplish that task and it's impossible to do it without Him.

I'm astounded by the multitude of people who take their health for granted, but I'm not surprised. I was exactly the same, running in overdrive as a working mom, youth group leader, hockey manager, wife, daughter, sister, and friend. I kept never-ending hours, barely slept, and then did it all again the next day. Until life knocked me on my butt. I was forced to make serious changes—which I wasn't pleased about at the time—that although didn't cure my condition, afforded me the quality of life required to continue putting one foot in front of the other.

Eating a natural diet, keeping physically fit, staying socially active, maintaining a positive attitude, and being a Christian have all kept me in healthy balance over the years and I know, without a doubt, they can do the same for you.

# WE FINALLY GET IT!

Chapter Twenty-Seven

THREE DECADES OF MONEY CONSERVATION HAVE WORKED well for Randy and I. As we reflect on the thriftiness we practiced over the years, we're definitely seeing the rewards of our efforts and indisputably and undeniably know God is blessing our finances. A number of years ago, my hubby and I reached the point in our Christian lives when we finally got the picture God can do way more with 90 percent of our earnings than we can do with 100 percent! We started to put the finishing touches on our tithing by joyously and prayerfully exceeding our 10 percent goal, donating to more Christ-centred organizations that were meaningful to us and humbly, usually privately, serving others in need.

We began to include our bank account in our daily prayers. We asked God to anoint our decisions, completely put our certainty in Him, and thanked Him profusely for all the blessings—and not just the financial ones—He provided on a daily basis. We embraced a mindset of sincere gratefulness, and finally, after years of trying to do it all on our own, became totally dependent on God for everything. Our greatest aspiration is to be life-speaking people of integrity with benevolent, servant hearts, and that through us; people will experience genuine compassion in Jesus' name.

I am honoured to say with God's guidance, my husband and I have become perfectly content and wholly fulfilled. We both have a close relationship with God, His Son, and the Holy Spirit, and live and breathe by the scripture that promises God intends for us to prosper. Whatever God has in store for the Leightons, we accept it. If our lives don't go in the direction we think they will, we are convinced God has another plan, a good plan, an even better plan than we can ever accomplish by ourselves.

Over the past twenty years, Randy and I have lost thousands of dollars in real estate transactions. This amount would throw any married couple into a tailspin of tears but we're flattered to be able to see a tiny part of our bigger picture that God personally handcrafted for us. What we have lost monetarily has been compensated with an exhaustive list of blessings from our Father including: my retired army man's acceptance back into the military, our child's protection during a serious, life-threatening illness, my job offer that came in a phone call (without a resume or interview), granting us children after the misery of infertility, saving two of our children's lives during their potentially fatal car accidents, and many, many others we assuredly aren't even aware of.

King David wrote: *"Faith shows the reality of what we hope for; it is the evidence of things we cannot see"* (Psalm 9:10). We know His name, trust Him implicitly, and He hasn't abandoned us. We are proud of our faith and belief in God's ability to watch over us, without thinking we have to intervene and give Him orders in His own jurisdiction. We feel like God is patting us on our heads and saying, *"… well done, my good and faithful servants…"* (paraphrased, Matthew 25:21).

It's true Randy and I have no way of recouping what we have lost during the sale of our homes but we have gained unfathomable wisdom and inner fulfillment in the process. We realize all the panicking we did over the years was fruitless. Our lives were riddled with unnecessary anxiety that would have easily vanished if we had just put all our reliance on God earlier on. We appreciate God goes before us to shield us from harm, stands behind us when we need Him most, and walks beside us every day of our life. He always has His hand out for us to hold and rest in the knowledge He is there for us. Always.

Finally free from worry, we understand God is in control, but not controlling us. He gives us the free will to make our own decisions and truly desires they line up with His Word. God never forces Himself on us. He allows us to make the mistakes we are determined to make, which often come with painful consequences, and then lovingly and patiently forgives us for our sins. He wants us to willingly come to Him and to transform our lives to be more like His flawless and sinless son Jesus.

The deeper the attachment we feel to God and personally benefit from the freedom that can only be found through Him, the less we wish to intentionally make harmful choices. Sin draws us away from God's protection and it's a desolate and deadly spot to be in. His love offers us comfort; a soothing relief from our tears, tranquility; a calmness that transcends all perception, a holy coat of armour; to protect us from danger, and faith; a complete confidence that we have a perfect place waiting for us in Heaven.

Through regular church attendance and group, as well as private study, Randy and I have learned God is sovereign—meaning He is the ruler and authority over all creation—and He is all-knowing (omniscient), all-powerful (omnipotent), and is everywhere at all times (omnipresent). We used to wonder why God would allow bad things to happen to good people, but we don't anymore. Hatred, cruelty, evil, and the abominations of mankind are not from God. They are a result of the sins of Adam and Eve in the Garden of Eden. God gave them the free will to make their own choices and only gave them one command. Adam and Eve freely chose to disobey God and that's when sin began. And now our civilization is full of it.

The human brain is not capable of deciphering God's almighty purpose. We can't figure out how God, who is the unequivocal definition of true love, can sit back and watch the pain and suffering that His people endure. But we can try to expand our views and beliefs and consider things from God's perspective. Those who have weathered life's atrocities gain the ability to help others who are undergoing the same. God can take any situation and work it out for good, positively changing the lives of others in the process. Affliction brings us into a deeper relationship with

God—He longs to be close to us and the tragedies that we endure do just that.

This sin-filled world we live in is not the end. It's just a blip on the timeline of eternity. The torment and sorrow we bear here on earth will all be washed away the moment we enter Heaven. There will be no more tears, no more sickness, and no more pain. We will exist in close fellowship with God, Jesus, and the Holy Spirit and will finally experience true, indescribable perfection.

We take the opportunity, as often as time permits, to impart all we've learned with Lucas, Jesse, and Devin. We hope they take the legacy of our mistakes, methods, and discoveries into careful consideration when developing their own spiritual and financial futures. As millennials, there are so many more ways to be both drawn away from God and economically wasteful than when we were young, and prayerfully our children will find their security in God, as opposed to their finances, by committing them to Him and trusting that He will always provide.

# CHANGING OUR MINDS

Chapter Twenty-Eight

AFTER WE SOLD OUR RETIREMENT HOME IN 2015, WE EMBARKED on a new adventure into the unknown. Randy had already been working away for three years and commuting every weekend. The kids moved on to adulthood, we sold half our belongings, reanalyzed our feelings about being tenants and moved back into the military housing units for the first time in nearly twenty years. We weren't sure how long we'd be stationed there and renting was a simple solution to avoid the imminent hassle of buying and selling in an already saturated market.

When we pulled the car up in front of our newly assigned unit, my eyes widened in disbelief. The dinky, old, run-down eyesore brought on the sting of apprehensive tears as I stared in fear. We had lived in modern, sizeable homes for so many years, I wasn't sure I was willing to return to the crowded neighbourhoods of the low-quality PMQs. I prayed to Jesus for encouragement as I unpacked our boxes. It was barely a flip of the calendar before we decided to look into the local real estate listings instead, as hubby and I kept bumping into each other and I was mortified to even invite someone over to our tiny, musty shack. Unbeknownst to us, God was in the middle of changing our hearts once again, and he was using that dreadful house to do it.

We excitedly ventured around town in search of a new place. Grasping that resale value was imperative, we drove into a new subdivision that offered custom stonework and stunning contemporary design. As our eyes feasted on the beautiful palaces, we imagined ourselves in their alluring open concepts and gigantic backyards, and called for a few quotes. Astronomical! Outrageous! Unthinkable! Oh my. Because Randy and I had already gone through the mentally draining feat of unrewarding real estate losses, we consciously determined we weren't willing to lay out that kind of cash again and commit to such a risky undertaking. We drove back to our dingy PMQ in defeat.

But something incredible happened as we opened our front door. What had originally appeared to us as trashy and embarrassing had now miraculously transfigured into quaint and affordable. As we'd wisely invested every cent from the sale of our home, the amount we were making in interest was more than enough to cover both our rent and utilities. The small size was easy to keep clean and we noticed that owning less stuff was freeing and fun. I still wasn't keen on having visitors though, until the day I got invited over for tea by a new friend from church. This woman rented the same style military quarters as us and the day I walked through her door, was the day my perspective changed forever.

Uncoordinated furniture filled the living room, the tea was served in chipped cups, and her three children were dressed in play clothes that didn't even match. She said she was taking an extended maternity leave from her job as a midwife and her husband was a doctor in the Air Force. They both grew up as children of missionaries and knew what it was like to live with lots of love but minimal things. As I slowly sipped my chamomile and watched her with her boys, my head exploded with revelation.

Things don't matter, fancy clothes are meaningless, and posh living conditions aren't essential. Face-to-face interactions are far superior to impersonal texts and a welcoming smile, mutual laughter, and warm genuine hugs are the authentic joys of life. My lowly, shabby house wasn't important and its appearance did not define me.

Even though my new friend and her hubby could have easily afforded a huge, Spanish Colonial in the posh area of town, they chose to live as minimalists and shared what they had with those less fortunate. That was the day my whole point of view changed. It became about people, not possessions. I started inviting other military girls over for coffee and even began a weekly ladies Bible study I'm still hosting today.

Randy is nearing retirement and we are making considerable progress in our arrangements for the next phase of our journey. Our initial notion was to have a 1,280 square-foot modular home built for the property we own in our hometown. But after hearing the price for that style, we had some major praying to do and choices to make. Our vision for retirement includes hanging out with our children, enjoying summers at the lake, and travelling far, far away from the cold Canadian winter. The original blueprint we'd selected won't allow for those goals but by downsizing another 200 square-feet and ordering a mini-home instead, we're saving almost $100,000!

Although we classify our current address as "cozy," we're going to have to seriously engage in some consciously creative storage and layout ideas because our new build is going to be even smaller. But as I've discovered over the last several years, houses don't matter, people do. We strive to show God's love to everyone we meet and I'm already laying the groundwork for hosting Bible study in our new living room, not forgetting of course, that we'll just have to sit much closer together.

# IT'S STILL GOOD

Chapter Twenty-Nine

You honestly won't believe it but I couldn't make this up if I tried. The knob on my crockpot has been broken for eleven months and I have to use pliers to turn it on and off. The plastic lids for our glass storage bowls are almost ripped beyond use, my food processor has been cracked for two drawn-out years, my favourite nightgown is practically threadbare (lucky Randy), and the cup for our mini-blender leaks a tad so if you don't drink fast, it drips out the bottom.

Our television broke during our last move so we're using the old el-cheapo from our camper, my dryer rudely burns our clothes if we don't monitor it vigilantly, my black dress boots have almost reached the point of disintegration in their eighth winter of use, our vacuum is held together by Velcro, and the floor fan in our bedroom has been leaning at a seventy-degree angle since last summer. Can we afford to replace everything? Of course we can. Do we need to get new ones yet? No, they're still good!

We laugh and thank God every time we use these things that they are still in functional condition. While we could easily compile an online order and have it all delivered within a few days, the longer we keep using these ones, the more money we'll have for something—or someone— more important. I often reminisce about the mentality of our grandparents. They would never entertain the thought of throwing something out unless it couldn't possibly be fixed, wouldn't dream of purchasing a new item without looking for a second-hand one first, took care of what they owned, never threw food in the garbage, and seemed content with what they had.

Such different ideals than the general population have today. We want what we want, exactly when we think we need it. There's no waiting, no saving, and no urge to buy anything less than the best. Many of today's newlyweds assume they must have, immediately after their wedding, a large, stylish house, with new appliances, updated siding, and a hot tub. Gone are the days of setting aside a portion of your wages, for months on end, to eventually be rewarded with the special item you needed. Credit card debt is at an all-time high and yet consumers continue to spend, spend, spend.

"I can't afford it" is a popular catchphrase today but what most really mean is that they refuse to curb the lifestyle they're accustomed to. I've heard forlorn students voice their concerns about increased tuition prices, unreasonable rental unit fees, and the colossal cost of textbooks. They spin a story of destitution and uncertainty while their feet are sporting three-hundred-dollar Australian boots, their body is covered with a goose-down jacket, and their teary eyes are enhanced by mile-long fake eyelashes. Much of the college crowd has maxed out all their cards and yet still somehow find the cash to congregate at the local pub for Friday night wings. Sadly, many adults find themselves in the same predicament but by then the devastation includes mortgages, electricity payments, and children.

Many in my military community claim they don't make enough money to cover the cost of their day-to-day needs. While I do agree that food and gas prices are higher than ever, basic budgeting can definitely enable families to manage within their paycheque and still put some away for later. There may be some that would hotly contest that fact but by simply being alert to your expenses and cutting unnecessary costs, it's still possible to not only survive, but successfully get ahead.

There's no denying we live in a self-indulgent culture. If our grandparents marvelled at a television remote and the microwave, just imagine what they would think about today's host of creature comforts.

The list of what today's money is wasted on is endless. While products of convenience can make our hectic lives easier, their old-fashioned counterparts cost significantly less and are just as effective. Working from the low end we have disposable makeup wipes, ready-to-heat meals, single-pod coffee machines, electronic book readers, Bluetooth speakers, and robot vacuums. We then graduate to weekly restaurant dates, monthly designer surprise boxes, garage door openers, remote car starters, home theatre systems with surround sound, gym equipment, hot tubs and swimming pools, and yearly resort vacations.

Anything and everything we want to make our life less stressful and enjoyable, we buy it! And while there's nothing wrong with owning these things after you've paid your bills, set aside a portion for your investments, and donated to a worthwhile charity, it's astounding how many people continue to find themselves deeper and deeper in debt.

On the flip side, I just had the honour of hearing a woman from our church recount the tale of her overseas medical mission trip. While it was inspiring to learn they treated hundreds of patients—for free—through their volunteer doctors, dentists, nurses, and everyday ordinary people, it was gut-wrenching to hear stories of women prostituting themselves to put food on their tables, men having to choose which of their children to sell in order to keep the rest of their family alive, and kids so malnourished that they are one breath away from death.

We live in a privileged society, there's no refuting that. And it's difficult for us to comprehend such desolation if we've never seen it with our own eyes. It's stories like this that put things into perspective. Why are we entitled to grumble about trivial things when there are so many around us that need our support? The Bible has a lot to say about helping the disadvantaged. The Apostle John says: *"If you have two shirts, give one to the poor. If you have food, share it with those who are hungry"* (Luke 3:11).

What hurts God's heart should break ours. Humanity is in a state of devastation. We have a duty to share what we have. There are hundreds of wonderful foundations that support those in need and I pray you feel called to aid in any way you can. Many charities assist individuals or villages overseas but if you wanted to give some of what you're favoured with here in your own neck of the woods, there are amazing organizations that do just that. I will list some tried and true charities at the back of the book for your consideration.

Speaking from hands-on experience, when we bless others, we are blessed in return. Randy and I have chosen to adopt this proverb as our life's motto: *"If you help the poor, you are lending to the Lord—and he will repay you!"* (Proverbs 19:17). It's critical to note poor doesn't just mean people without money; it includes the addicted, the abused, the sick, and the abandoned.

We all have something to give. Take a look around your home. Can you afford to spare a little to help the underprivileged? While giving doesn't always mean contributing your money, it can certainly change a life. It's impossible for us to change the whole world but we can make a difference, one soul at a time. You could prayerfully give to your local food bank, mental health centre, homeless shelter, or go online and choose a child to sponsor in an impoverished country. You could also volunteer your time. If you're really feeling called to take action in a more concrete way, soup kitchens, boys and girls clubs, or Habitat for Humanity and Samaritan's Purse are all about hands-on work.

We can all remember the warm glow we have felt when we've truly helped another human being; the pure, unexplainable joy of lending a hand and being rewarded with heartfelt thanks. Be free with your kind words, generosity, and love. We only get one life, let's live it to the fullest and equip someone else to do the same.

# THE
# LATER YEARS

Chapter Thirty

THE LIFE STORY OF A CHRISTIAN CONSISTS OF A "BEFORE" AND
an "after"; living for themselves before inviting Jesus into
their heart and living for God and the needs of His people
afterwards. I think I was around twelve years old when I
promised to live my life for Jesus and spent the next couple
of decades thinking I was a good person. But to be embarrassingly candid, there were a few instances in my past
when I wasn't very good at all. Sure, I went to church,
was nice enough to others, and never broke any laws, but
once in a while I engaged in self-sabotaging behaviour,
was negative and envious, and now and again selfish and
judgemental. I've always considered myself to be an honest
person but there were many times over the years I wasn't
honest with myself. Dabbling in sin, I was justifying my

actions by thinking that if others were acting that way, why couldn't I?

I occasionally felt convicted over my actions but would scoff and brush them off as no big deal. But the reason I had to stop acting like everyone else was because I *wasn't* like everyone else. When I became a Christian, I was sanctified (set apart) for God's purpose. While it would take many years of trial and error to discover my true calling, the more my behaviour emulated the world, the more I sensed God telling me to stop. He said no more bitterness, no more envy, no more self-pity, and no more shame.

In the course of my maturity, He has developed qualities in me that aren't just indicative of a good person. Everyone thinks they're a good person but only God gets to make that judgement, and I aim to do all that I can to follow His Word and make Him proud.

It causes me unspeakable remorse to say that Randy and I took the long way around to putting all, not just some or most, of our faith in Jesus. We now know that He is our Rock, our Advocate, our Redeemer, and our Saviour. Everything about our former lives has changed. While we still like to have a good time, we have redefined what having a good time means. We are consistently cautious with the music we listen to and the movies we watch and are careful when we are out and about to be wary of any influence that might draw us away from God. We are conscientious of our actions and apologize when needed, give forgiveness where forgiveness is due, and are working on being *"...quick to listen, slow to speak, and slow to get angry"* (James 1:19).

Randy and I don't have a clear indication of where our future will take us, and that's okay. We are comfortable resting in each and every one of God's promises we find in our Bible and keeping His ways and directions as our primary objective. We trust that whatever may come our way, whether it coincides with our dreams or not, God will be right there with us, holding our hands and guiding the way.

Many of my lunch mates over the years have questioned why I don't open my fortune cookie after a Chinese meal. While I know they're just for fun—and if I use the lucky numbers I'll definitely strike it rich—I believe, without question, my eternity is already secure because the Bible says: *"Seek the Kingdom of God above all else, and live righteously, and he will give you everything you need"* (Matthew 6:33).

My principal prayer is that our children will follow Jesus with unwavering devotion and delight in all the kingdom of God has to offer them, and that tasteless, crumbly, Magic 8 Ball-of-a-cookie doesn't have the power to grant that request. Only God can do that.

Because we meticulously invested and calculated for retirement, Randy and I are able to fully retire by age 50. Years of financial conversations and revelations have drawn us to the conclusion that we would love, more than anything, to share our savings and earnings with our children before we die. This does sound a little premature, even to my ears, as we assuredly aren't even anywhere close to being classified as old yet, however, this matter is very dear to our hearts and is one of the most important financial resolutions we have made to date. It will give us immense pleasure to watch our children and grandchildren enjoy their inheritance before we go to Heaven as opposed to just leaving it to them in a will after we're gone.

While these funds won't be anywhere near a vast fortune in which our kids will never have to work again, it will be our honour to gently help Lucas, Jesse, and Devin with their first homes, education funds for their children, and our future grandchildren's music and swimming lessons. As we definitely don't intend on instilling a spirit of expectancy and reliance in our children that Gramma and

Grampa will pay for everything and that they can just blow their cash on silly and unnecessary stuff, Randy and I will be sure to carefully ponder and pray together over these decisions as they arise in the next few years.

# THE JOURNEY CONTINUES

Chapter Thirty-One

WITH A LITTLE ASSISTANCE FROM MY UPBRINGING AND A LOT of help from God, I've saved our family well over $100,000 throughout the past 29 years. I started out on my own, thinking I was the master of my own destiny and was totally capable of handling and deflecting any rocky situation that came my way. Headstrong and defiant, I unknowingly rejected God and His incredible plan for me. After years of trial and error, tears and pain, mistakes and forgiveness, and prayers and blessings, I've accomplished my deep-rooted ambition of finally putting God first.

For my last birthday I got a tattoo that says "I AM SECOND." I prayerfully contemplated the idea of getting it for many years but just mustered up the courage to get inked. It's both a visible reminder to me that my life is not about me and a public statement to others that I'm a child of God. He is my first priority. I hope I can share my experiences with others, my demeanour will be a living role model for Christianity, and God continues to guide me on the mission He's deliberately prepared for me.

For some unknown reason, I've always felt the need to justify my actions, my speech, my child-rearing skills, my morals and principles, my beliefs, and my money management methods. The completion of this book has closed that chapter of my self-doubt and while I will never stop changing and growing, I stand strong knowing I am the person I've always aspired to be, a confident, fearless, bold woman of God.

I pray I inspire others to be all God's created them to be and bask in the contentment of recognizing they are truly loved. We really don't require anything other than God, because when we have Him close by, everything else falls into place. As long as I'm working for Him here on earth, and loving and caring about His people, I know He stands behind me like a proud father, cheering me on.

For many years, I've wondered what my gift is and what the true meaning of life is. While I've come close a few times to figuring out what my divine purpose is, I feel compelled to keep seeking, searching, and exploring the wonderful world God has put before me until the day I get to meet Him face-to-face. My hands are to touch the hearts of others, lead home Bible studies, and love like Jesus does. My feet are for meeting women at the coffee shop who hunger for a compassionate ear, walking a mile in another's shoes, and continuing on the narrow path God has designed specifically for me.

I pray I have shed some much-needed light on the indescribable relationship with God that's available to everyone who calls on His name. A life with Jesus in it won't be without difficulty and distress, but I guarantee you'll be comforted in understanding that He will always be with you and you'll never be alone. This verse has never failed to encourage the low in spirit: *"So be strong and courageous! Do not be afraid and do not panic before them. For the Lord your God will personally go ahead of you. He will neither fail you nor abandon you"* (Deuteronomy 31:6).

It's freeing to break the chains of your past, leave your old ways behind and embark on an exciting journey of spiritual awakening with God that will forever change the way you think, feel, and act. The Apostle Paul explained to the Corinthians: *"This means that anyone who belongs to Christ has become a new person. The old life is gone; a new life has begun!"* (2 Corinthians 5:17)

I earnestly pray this book will open the eyes of those who don't already know God; ignite curiosity in people who have heard about Him but have never taken the next step; give strength to those who are in the midst of adversity and despair; and renew passion and commitment to Christians who already know and follow Him.

We live on a visually stunning planet but constantly overlook its majesty in pursuit of something more. Like I did for years, many people concentrate on just surviving. They rise every morning to a chaotic and maddening human rat race and wearily endure the burdens and headaches of our modern day society. They work tirelessly on their happiness and go to bed dreaming of bigger and better. Constantly obsessing about the future and what treasures or tragedies it may hold for them, they never take the opportunity to slow down, count their blessings, and be grateful for everything they already have.

I've had the honour of watching a number of ladies that attended my Bible study invite Jesus into their lives and become Christians. But what actually is a Christian? A Christian is defined as a follower of Jesus Christ. They believe Jesus is God's Son, that He died for our sins on the cross, and then came back to life three days later. The mark of a true Christian is loving God with all your heart, soul, and mind, and loving others. We know that the Holy Bible is the true Word of God and its presence both protects us from suffering and enriches every aspect of our being.

To some, the Bible may sound like a strict set of rules making you give up all the fun things you get tangled up in, but the guidelines in the Bible are there to help us, not harm us, and please be honest, do all those things you engage in really enhance your life? Is the bottle actually worth the hangover? Does the self-pity you engage in actually improve your mindset? Is the "ravish me" movie implanting ideals in your head that your spouse can never live up to? Do all these things really make you feel better or do they just mask what's missing?

The void in our hearts can only be filled with the love of God. Please hear me when I tell you that I tried, with all my might, to fill that void with other things, but was never, ever successful. God is our Heavenly Father, and like our earthly fathers, He wants to protect His children from mistakes that lead to regret. He knew you before you were even born and has a good plan already predetermined for you. The Lord knows your innermost thoughts and your soul, loves you with His perfect love, and wishes to have a relationship with you. It's never too late. You only need to call out to Him.

If you are curious about life as a Christian, I invite you to turn to the back of the book to find out what to do to be free from the past and walk into your new and improved life with God, Jesus, and the Holy Spirit, and get to live forever and ever in Heaven.

If you've already made a commitment to Jesus once before but find you've reverted to a few of your old sense-less ways, it's time to rededicate your life. Turn to the back of the book and take the necessary steps to get back on track. I've shared some valuable resources for all, regardless of where you currently are in your faith. If you're already living your life as a Christian, that's so great. I'm privileged to be a part of God's family with you and pray you'll stand strong in your faith, attend a Bible-based church, study His Word, and love others with everything you've got!

It is God's desire we trust in Him and live our lives as His content sons and daughters. We are to place all our faith in Him and thrive, not just survive, in this awe-inspiring world. While I don't know what my future will hold and where my adventures with God will take me, I believe I'm a beloved daughter of my King and no matter what happens, one day I will walk hand in hand with Him, together forever in Heaven...and I hope to see you there.

# APPENDICES

## What on Earth Is a Christian?

A Christian is a person who:

1. is kind to everyone (even when people aren't kind to them)
2. maintains a positive attitude (even when they're having a bad day)
3. is quick to apologize (even when they don't want to)
4. doesn't hold grudges (forgives easily)
5. is unselfish (putting the needs of others before theirs)
6. accepts the faults in others (and still likes them anyway)

7. leads a peaceful life (gentleness and graciousness are key)
8. is generous (with their time, love, money, and kind words)
9. is slow to get angry (no complaining, arguing, rude remarks)
10. practices gratitude in all situations (even the bad ones)
11. is not judgemental (treats everyone the same)
12. never talks about others behind their back (ever)

LOVES GOD     LOVES PEOPLE     LOVES LIFE

## What Is Prayer?

Prayer is a conversation with God. He knows your needs before you even speak them but He loves you and longs to hear your voice. We can pray anywhere at any time and there isn't a right or wrong way to do it. It doesn't have to be complicated. Prayer gives us an opportunity to open our hearts to Jesus who then takes our request to His Father on our behalf. We can talk to Him about anything: a decision we need help with, a friend that's hurting, a worry on our mind, or a toothache that just won't go away. Ask God for wisdom during tough times, who He would like you to comfort, to keep your family safe, and for forgiveness when you've made a mistake. Always remember to be grateful to God for everything He provides.

Over time, prayer becomes as natural as breathing. We can talk to Jesus while driving, resting, or working. He hears your short, quick prayer the same as He receives your lengthy tear-filled one. God delights in our voice and wants to hear it more often. Just remember to thank Him when He answers your prayer and thank Him even more when He doesn't!

## The Christian Life

### What a Christian Believes

- Jesus is the sinless son of God; He was fully man and is fully God.
- Jesus died for the sin of the world (and ours) and was resurrected three days later.
- God, Jesus, and the Holy Spirit form one God in three persons.
- The Bible is the Word of God.

### Qualities of a Christian

- "Taken off their old life" and "put on" a new one—being "born again"
- Have a personal relationship with God, Jesus, and the Holy Spirit.
- Behaviour is reflective of a follower of Jesus Christ.

### How to Become a Christian

- Make an informed decision to become a Christian.

- Pray to God (sinner's prayer below) and commit your whole life to Him.
- Receive Jesus, by faith, fully trusting He's your Saviour.

### Sinner's Prayer

There are two parts to the sinner's prayer. The Bible says *"Everyone who calls on the name of the Lord will be saved"* (Romans 10:13). Everyone, that means YOU!

In Romans we read:

*If you openly declare that Jesus is Lord and believe in your heart that God raised him from the dead, you will be saved. For it is by believing in your heart that you are made right with God, and it is by openly declaring your faith that you are saved.*

—Romans 10:9-10

It's important to note God is not mad at you. He loves you. The slate of your life and your sins will be wiped clean the moment you enter God's family. The Bible says God loves us so much He sent His one and only Son Jesus to shed His blood and die on the cross for our sins and then raised Him from the dead on the third day after His death.

If you want to become a Christian and live in Heaven for eternity, say these words out loud:

"Dear God, I want to be a part of your family. I know I have sinned, please forgive me. I acknowledge that Your Son Jesus died for my sins on the cross, You raised Him from the dead, and I accept Him into my life as my Lord and Saviour. Amen."

Congratulations, you're a Christian! Now what?

- Tell someone about your newfound faith in Jesus Christ
- Spend time with God each day—praying to Him and reading your Bible
- Find a Bible-based church and attend regularly
- Make friends with other Christians and ask them to support you in your new life
- Get baptized—this makes a public declaration of your faith and commitment

## Rededication to God

If you have dedicated your life to God in the past but have reverted back to some of your old ways, fallen away from Him, or just want to recommit yourself to your Christian walk, say this prayer:

> "Dear God, please forgive me. I let myself get drawn away from the path you set out for me but I'm ready to get back on track. Thank you for sending Your son, Jesus to die on the cross for me and then bringing Him back to life. I will accept the Spirit's guidance and return to living according to Your Word. Amen"

## Helpful Resources

We all have questions; it's a natural part of being human. What's your favourite colour? When will you be home? Why can't you hit the laundry basket? While these all require simple, one-word responses (well, maybe not the one about the laundry basket), what about the answers to questions that can't be immediately explained? How will I get out of debt? How can I stop worrying? What's the meaning of life? What is my true purpose? Undoubtedly, these are mysterious queries that can kidnap your thoughts and mess up your sleep.

While the Internet is a mind-blowing tool of unsurpassable intelligence, I can't stress enough to be vigilant about where you get your information. If I believed every tidbit of weird information I found on my quest to cure my disorder, I'd have taken out shares in sinus decongestant or be covered in bee stings. I'm pleased to share what's been helpful for our family over the years and hope you'll check them out.

## Reading Material

- *The Purpose Driven Life*—Rick Warren
- *The Wealthy Barber* and *The Wealthy Barber Returns*—David Chilton
- *Money Sense* magazine (available online)

## Websites

- gotquestions.org (answers to EVERY question you can possibly have about God)
- focusonthefamily.ca (covering a range of topics from marriage to finances)
- daveramsey.com (real solutions for freedom from financial stress)

## Sharing with Others

### International

- Samaritan's Purse: a nondenominational Christian organization (run by the family of Billy Graham) that helps meet the physical and spiritual needs of victims of war, poverty, natural disasters, and disease all over the world

- Compassion International: child development organization working to end poverty in the lives of children and their families in Jesus' name

- World Vision: global relief, development and advocacy organization that partners with children, families, and communities to tackle causes of poverty and injustice

### Canadian

- Teen Challenge: a faith-based residential drug and alcohol rehabilitation program helping teens and adults overcome addiction and lead full and healthy lives (also international)

- Salvation Army: a ministry motivated by the love of God that works to meet human need without discrimination (also international)
- Focus on the Family: Christian organization providing all families with the necessary resources to help and keep families together in today's complicated world (also North America-wide)

Local (depending on your area):
- Soup kitchens
- Pregnancy centres
- Food banks